Wounded Personalities
A Practical Guide to Understanding Personality Disorders
Gregory Pacana

"It is easier to build strong children than to repair broken men."

— *Frederick Douglass*

Disclaimer

The diagnostic terms used in this book are in no way meant to insult, embarrass, or to label anyone. Terms such as borderline, schizoid, and narcissist are the currently accepted terms used by the psychiatric community. They are used in this book as a way of conveying information and describing types of behavior. It would be virtually impossible to write an articulate book about this subject matter without using these terms. However, human beings are not their diagnoses and they are not defined by their disorders.

Secondly, when reading about the causes of the conditions discussed in this book, there may be a temptation by some to assign blame to parents, perhaps to mothers in particular. However, to do so would be a mistake. There is a huge difference between understanding where a particular set of behaviors may have come from and blaming someone for them. One is called *insight* and that is a healthy step on the road to healing. The other is called *excuse making* and that is a convenient and guaranteed way to remain stuck. While it may feel good to blame someone else for our current circumstances, it does nothing to advance the conversation or to promote the healing process. Blaming others for our problems or deficits is simply a waste of time.

With regard to the DSM psychiatric conditions, symptoms and diagnoses referenced in this book, the reader must keep in mind the following: "The diagnostic criteria have been included in the DSM because their provision has been shown to increase diagnostic agreement. It is important to understand that the appropriate use of the diagnostic criteria requires clinical training and that they cannot be simply applied in a cookbook fashion. The primary purpose of the DSM is to facilitate communication among mental health professionals. The diagnostic terms in the manual provide convenient shorthand when communicating about patients."

Finally, the information presented in this book comes from the author's personal experiences with friends, acquaintances, in dating situations, with family members, and in romantic relationships. In addition, much of the information has come from formal classroom training, and through reading books and articles from others who work in the field of psychology and psychiatry. A significant amount of the information presented in this book has been adapted from the Author's own original articles, which have been published on the *Examiner.com* platform.

Contents

Dad and his sister Phyllis home from the Orphanage in 1946

Dedication
To Dad:

This book is lovingly dedicated to my late father, Philip Pacana (1938-2001). Dad spent his early childhood, from 1939 until 1946, growing up in an orphanage in Coatesville, Pa. Despite the fact that it was a caring Catholic orphanage it was certainly not a suitable substitute for being raised in a home with a loving mother and father.

He left the orphanage in 1946, at the age of eight and returned home to Philadelphia where he was reunited with his mother and his three siblings. He went on to graduate from Saint Michael's grade school and Northeast public high school.

He met my mother, Maryann, in 1959 when he was twenty-one and they were married in 1962. They went on to have three children, my older sister Helene, myself, and my younger sister, Lisa. We lived an upper middle class existence and never really wanted for anything. Dad was a good father, a hard worker, and an excellent provider. We all attended Catholic grade school and Catholic high school. I would go on to attend college as well.

While for the most part Dad was very normal there always seemed to be something missing in him. It was hard for us to understand at the time but looking back it was as if he was lacking something emotionally. It was difficult for my mother, my sisters, and I to form a strong loving connection with him.

My father passed away in February 2001 after a long battle with colon cancer. Even when he was dying and drifting in and out of consciousness, he would make references to those early years and events that took place during his time in the orphanage.

It was not until many years later when I began studying psychology that some of the pieces about Dad began to fall into place. I learned about an *ego-syntonic* psychiatric condition known as NPD or narcissistic personality disorder, and to me that sounded a lot like Dad.

Dad could be boastful when it came to his accomplishments as well as his appearance. He would come across to others as being superior and even obnoxious at times. He was very competitive, even with us, his three children. However, most significantly, he had a difficult time connecting with us emotionally. That all-important human emotion known as *empathy* seemed to be lacking in him.

For me this was never as evident as when, at the age of nineteen, I was diagnosed with cancer. I was forced to leave college during my first year and endured two surgeries and eighteen grueling months of aggressive chemotherapy. While my mother was at my side through it all, Dad was astonishingly missing. Not only was it rare for him to spend time with me at the hospital, but he never had anything to say to me in the way of support, encouragement, or reassurance. He was emotionally absent during my entire battle with cancer.

Whether or not my father was truly a *clinical narcissist*, I suppose I can never know for sure. I did come to learn that this condition is more prevalent among individuals who are raised in orphanages than in a loving family environment. Not a single day goes by when I do not think about him. Given what I have learned about personality disorders and clinical narcissism, I have a newfound compassion for this man. Contrary to what we once believed, today the consensus regarding narcissism is that this disorder is the result in part of a childhood marked by neglect and a lack of maternal bonding.

Therefore, this book is dedicated to my father who, like so many other children who endured a harsh childhood marked by trauma and abandonment, went on to develop a *wounded personality*.

The Casualties

According to the most recent data available from the Department of Health & Human Services, there are nearly 680,000 victims of childhood abuse and neglect in the United States each year. This number equates to approximately nine in every 1,000 American children. Nationally, 79.5 percent of these children were neglected, 18 percent were physically abused, 9.0 percent were sexually abused, and another 8.7 percent were psychologically abused. In addition, over 1,500 American children died because of abuse and neglect in 2013.

Victims in their first year of life had the highest rate of victimization at 23 per 1,000 children. The majority of victims consisted of three races or ethnicities—White (44.0%), Hispanic (22.4%), and African-American (21.2%).

In the vast majority of these cases, over 80%, a biological parent was the perpetrator of the abuse/neglect. Four-fifths (83.0%) of perpetrators were between the ages of 18 and 44 years. More than one-half (53.9%) of perpetrators were women, and 45.0 percent of perpetrators were men. The three largest percentages of perpetrators were White (49.3 %), African-American (20.1%), or Hispanic (19.5%).

This trauma includes physical, emotional, sexual, and psychological abuse. Many of these children will grow to become adults with serious psychological and emotional problems. In the most severe cases, about nine percent, these children will grow into adults with a clinical personality disorder.

Therefore, this book is dedicated in part to the unfortunate American children who have grown into adults with damaged and *wounded personalities.*

Foreword

I am a Board Certified Psychiatrist and Board Certified Psychoanalyst. I am also a Training Analyst at the Institute of the Psychoanalytic Center of Philadelphia, and have been in the private practice of psychiatry and psychoanalysis for over 40 years. I first met Gregory Pacana in 1992, when at the age of 28 he was working as a computer specialist for the federal government. He was a very bright young man and a valued employee and his career was on the fast track, but he suffered with moderately severe depression and anxiety.

Gregory had been diagnosed with cancer at age 19, but after two surgeries and aggressive chemotherapy, he survived both the cancer and the treatment. He also had survived a difficult childhood in which both parents had a difficult time nurturing their children.

Gregory became deeply involved in his psychotherapy as he tried to unravel the causes of his anxiety and depression and sought to understand the forces, which had been at work in forming his own personality, as well as the personalities of his parents and his siblings. Gregory showed an unusual aptitude for psychological understanding both of complex psychological concepts and of the therapeutic processes involved in healing the deep psychological wounds from his past.

At the age of 38, Gregory suffered a brain hemorrhage, which left him paralyzed on his left side. He was confined to a wheelchair for nearly a year. He went through an arduous period of rehabilitation, and eventually made an almost miraculous recovery. He left his job with the federal government and set out to reinvent himself. He decided to go back to school to study psychology. He also began a writing career. He published his first article in 2010, and then went on to write for three different local newspapers, then a series of over 200 online articles. His writing, including his writing in this book, demonstrates his ability to take difficult psychological concepts and make them accessible to the average person. He has helped many people over the years with his articles and through a Facebook page followed by over 7000 fans.

Wounded Personalities seeks to explain what is meant by the psychological concept "personality disorder." In this book, Gregory has managed to synthesize all the pieces of his growing understanding of these personality disorders, beginning with an understanding of the vital importance of attachment and empathy to the growing child and the poisonous effect of shame to the developing *Self*. He explains the various signs of personality disorders in a way that helps us to recognize these traits in others or in ourselves. He also explains the process of healing that must occur if we are to allow ourselves to develop in healthier ways. His explanations are clear and aimed at helping the general population to understand this very complex aspect of mental health.

Edward Livingston Hicks, M.D.
Psychiatrist and Psychoanalyst

Preface

All human behavior can be understood by applying the question, *"What need is being met with the behavior or what belief about myself am I attempting to reinforce?"* Whether it is the simple act of getting a drink of water to quench one's thirst, someone choosing to adopt a pet to alleviate feelings of loneliness, or self-medicating with alcohol to numb feelings of despair and emptiness there is always a *payoff* for the individual.

The point is human beings do not engage in positive, negative, or even self-destructive behavior without there being some type of personal payoff. Once we begin to look at behavior and even symptoms as coping mechanisms or methods for fulfilling unmet needs, the behaviors cease to be a mystery and instead begin to make sense as a necessary method for satisfying one's needs.

While reading this book the reader will be presented with clinical disorders with accompanying symptoms. With each symptom, the reader should attempt to understand the function of the symptom in terms of filling *unmet needs* or reinforcing *long held beliefs*.

Along these lines, there is a term used in psychology called "prophecy fulfillment." It essentially means, confirming what we already believe to be true about ourselves. Human beings will go to extraordinary measures to ensure prophecy fulfillment in their lives. When we hold a belief about ourselves, whether it is positive, negative, true, or false we will engage in behaviors that will reinforce that belief.

In order to demonstrate prophecy fulfillment we need look no further than the personality disorder known as BPD or borderline personality disorder. People who suffer with this disorder have the long held belief that others will eventually abandon or leave them. The most prominent symptom of BPD is the *fear of abandonment*. The irony is that those with borderline personality will themselves often be the cause of the abandonment with their frantic, clingy, and erratic behavior towards their partner, thus fulfilling their long-held belief of abandonment. (i.e., prophecy fulfillment)

In a similar manner, narcissists hold the essential belief that they are superior to others. Many of the symptoms associated with narcissism including their need for admiration, their grandiosity, and their tendency to elevate themselves by devaluing others reinforces the narcissist's belief or "ego coping mechanism" that he is in fact superior to others.

In order to understand negative behavior as well as clinical symptoms we need to begin to see behavior as filling an unmet need in the individual. Once we can view clinical symptoms and behaviors as *ego defense mechanisms* as opposed to abnormal behavior, the mystery of the symptoms disappears and the possibility for change can begin.

Introduction

Psychology is one of the social sciences, which deals with the study of human behavior and mental processes. Psychiatry on the other hand is a physical science, which deals with the diagnosis and treatment of mental disorders. Psychiatrists are doctors who have chosen to specialize in the field of mental health. Psychologists are not doctors; they are scientists who have completed some degree of course work in the field of psychology (Associate, Bachelors, Masters, or Doctorate).

This book deals with concepts based both in psychology and psychiatry and it is not unusual for there to be an overlap in these two disciplines. Remember, psychiatrists are physicians first who have graduated from medical school and are licensed to prescribe medication; most often, they prescribe psychiatric medications. Oftentimes a psychologist will work in tandem with a psychiatrist primarily for prescribing an antidepressant or anti-anxiety medication for a client.

This book focuses on an area in abnormal psychology known as *personality disorders*. In both psychology and psychiatry, personality disorders are a special kind of mental health condition. The mental health conditions which most people are familiar with; things such as depression, anxiety, and bipolar disorder are referred to as *ego-dystonic* disorders meaning "something which is inconsistent with oneself." With ego-dystonic disorders, a person feels the discomfort

11

from the disorder and realizes that something is wrong. In many cases, they will then seek out treatment. That is much different from personality disorders, which are *ego-syntonic*.

Ego-syntonic refers to "a condition or state of being that is consistent with oneself." In other words, the individual generally does not feel as if anything is wrong with them. This is primarily true because our personalities have been with us our entire lives and they are all that we know.

Another feature of personality disorders is that they generally will not respond to treatment. This is not to say that some improvements cannot be made in motivated courageous individuals but these improvements tend to be marginal and they can take a long time to achieve

This book is intended to help the nonprofessional understand the complexities of several major personality disorders. It is not meant to be a diagnostic tool; it is rather a guide to help individuals gain an understanding of the origin and symptoms of several of the most debilitating personality disorders.

After reading this book, it is my sincere hope that the reader will walk away with a genuine understanding of borderline personality disorder, narcissistic personality disorder, histrionic personality disorder, avoidant personality disorder, schizoid personality disorder, dependent personality disorder, and codependent personality. It is also my hope that for those individuals that suffer with these disorders or their "traits" that this book might be a possible first step in the *healing process*. Despite what conventional psychiatry suggests regarding the long-term prognosis for these disorders some degree of healing is always possible in determined individuals with insight.

 In addition, while many will argue the precise cause of personality disorders, the connection between childhood neglect/abuse and later developing a wounded or damaged personality seems undeniable.

Chapter 1: What is a personality disorder?

Our personality makes us unique; in many ways, it defines us. Our individual personality determines how we think, feel, and behave. Personality determines how we experience both our inner world (our thoughts and feelings) and our outer world (our behavior and our interactions with others). Our personalities are a result of both biological and social factors.

The most widely accepted theory for measuring human personality is known as the "Big Five" theory developed in the 1970s by American psychologist Lewis Goldberg. According to Goldberg and others, human personality can be understood through the application of five broad dimensions. They are conscientiousness, openness, agreeableness, neuroticism, and extraversion. Studies have shown that these five dimensions are universal and apply to all cultures, races, and ethnicities.

These five broad dimensions can best be understood as existing in all of us, but in a matter of degree. They can also be looked at as pairs of opposites, i.e., extroversion vs. introversion, openness vs. close-mindedness, neuroticism vs. emotional stability, agreeableness vs. unfriendliness, and conscientiousness vs impulsiveness.

Fortunately, most people have a healthy "normal" personality. This is evident by their ability to hold jobs, enjoy rich social lives, and have satisfying relationships (both romantic and platonic). However, for the unfortunate few, roughly nine percent, this is not the case. Biological factors (the genes from their mother and father) and social factors (early childhood experiences with caregivers) have come together to create a damaged or impaired personality. Psychiatrists refer to these damaged personalities as clinical personality disorders.

A personality disorder is diagnosed when an individual experiences significant impairment in their social or occupational functioning and when the individual's manner of thinking, feeling, or behaving causes them significant distress. In the simplest terms having a personality disorder means that an individual's manner of thinking, feeling, and behaving causes them distress or ongoing problems with occupation and relationships.

"Personality disorders, such as borderline are sculpted by our earliest relationship experiences. Those imprints shape how we feel about ourselves and determine the extent to which we are able to forge trust in others. Much of borderline distress occurs within the first year of life, due to inadequate bonding and emotional attunement with the mother. " — *Shari Schreiber, M.A.*

Generally, psychiatry recognizes ten personality disorders. They are:

1. **Paranoid personality disorder**: Paranoid PD is characterized by feelings of extreme distrust, being

overly guarded, and suspiciousness of others.

2. **Schizoid personality disorder**: Schizoid PD is characterized by being detached, aloof, and lacking in emotional response.

3. **Schizotypal disorder**: Schizotypal PD is characterized by oddities in appearance, behavior, and speech and magical thinking.

4. **Antisocial personality disorder**: Antisocial PD is characterized by a lack of remorse and a callous disregard for the rights of others. (*Also referred to as sociopathy or psychopathy*)

5. **Borderline personality disorder**: Borderline PD is characterized by fears of abandonment, emotional instability, and impulsive behavior.

6. **Histrionic personality disorder**: Histrionic PD is characterized by dramatic and attention seeking behavior.

7. **Narcissistic personality disorder**: Narcissistic PD is characterized by grandiose thinking, an excessive need for admiration, and a lack of empathy.

8. **Avoidant personality disorder**: Avoidant PD is characterized by intense feelings of inadequacy and social inhibition.

9. **Dependent personality disorder**: Dependent PD is characterized by an extreme lack of self-confidence, submissive behavior, and an excessive need to be taken care of.

10. **Obsessive-compulsive personality disorder:** Obsessive-compulsive PD is characterized by extreme orderliness, perfectionism, and rituals.

These ten disorders are normally grouped into three clusters as follows:

The *Cluster A personalities* are referred to as the *Odd or Eccentric* personalities and include schizotypal, schizoid and paranoid personality disorders.

The *Cluster B personalities* are referred to as the *Dramatic* personalities and include borderline, antisocial, histrionic, and narcissistic personality disorders.

The *Cluster C personalities* are referred to as the *Anxious* personalities and include avoidant, dependent and obsessive-compulsive personality disorders.

It is important to keep in mind when reading this book that having a clinical personality disorder is not the same as being eccentric, unconventional, or odd. In addition, individuals with personality disorders are not weak in character, lacking in self-control, selfish, or intentionally malevolent. People with personality disorder sometimes have a difficult time getting along with others. They may even be hostile, manipulative, and demanding. However, their behavior is not intentional in the strictest sense. They are genuinely impaired in the manner in which they think, feel, and behave. There are observable physiological differences in the brains of these individuals. They cannot just *"get over it."*

Personality disorders are real medical and psychiatric illnesses. They are *neurological* and based in science and medicine. Moreover, they are not something people choose to have, and currently they cannot be cured. In many cases, they can be managed and symptoms can be treated but there is no cure for personality disorders This book will examine borderline, narcissistic, histrionic, avoidant, schizoid, and dependent personalities. In addition, we will examine a personality type that is not recognized as a clinical personality disorder, *codependent personality*. Codependency was considered for inclusion as a personality disorder in 1987 but the decision was made to not to list it in the Diagnostic and Statistical Manuel since many of the traits associated with codependency are often highly beneficial in occupational and social functioning. Borderline personality disorder will receive more attention in this book than the other personality disorders. Borderline personality is arguably the most devastating of the personality disorders. It is now believed that as many as six percent of the adult population, roughly 10 million Americans, suffer with BPD. This translates to roughly 1 in 15 American adults. That means that we all know at least one person who suffers with BPD.

We also know that borderline personality is no longer a predominantly female disorder, as men are just as likely to suffer with it, but perhaps with a slightly different symptom presentation. Borderline personality is also associated with self-injury, primarily in the form of either self-cutting or self-burning. In addition, it has one of the highest mortality rates of any mental health condition. Unlike some of the other personality disorders, the connection between this disorder and early childhood abuse, neglect, and even sexual abuse is well established. These individuals therefore have been particularly wounded at a young age.

It is also important when reading this book to remember that there is a significant difference between qualifying for a diagnosis of a personality disorder and having *traits* of a particular personality disorder. Many people have borderline or narcissistic traits yet they do not meet the diagnostic criteria for the clinical personality disorder.

For instance if someone is impulsive, fears being alone, and is prone to mood swings we might say they have *borderline traits*. If someone is arrogant, grandiose, and has a sense of entitlement, we could say they have *narcissistic traits*. To have traits of one, two, or more personality disorders is common, but to meet the clinical diagnosis of a personality disorder is relatively rare.

The reader must be careful *not* to make the mistake of diagnosing themselves or others. Even if an individual seems to have all the symptoms of a particular disorder, it still does not mean they qualify for the clinical diagnosis.

The diagnosis of a personality disorder is a difficult one to make and it can only be made by a qualified mental health professional who is experienced in diagnosing and treating these relatively rare psychiatric disorders.

Chapter 2: Core damaged children

Adults who were abused or neglected as children are lacking an essential part of themselves. They suffer from what are referred to in the psychological community as, *core damage issues*. The term core damage refers to the type of psychological trauma that occurs during infancy or in early childhood and affects every aspect of one's life. Children with core damage are much more likely to have emotional problems as adults and are at an increased risk for developing a clinical personality disorder.

Individuals with core damage issues tend to have similar characteristics or psychological symptoms. Since they suffered emotional or physical neglect as children, their adult behaviors are very much the same and often include the following adaptive behaviors.

Common behaviors seen in adults with core damage:

- Judging themselves very harshly
- Perfectionism
- Putting the needs of others ahead of their own
- Low self-esteem and feelings of inadequacy
- Seeking the approval of others (people-pleasing)
- Very sensitive to criticism
- A feeling that they are very different from others
- Over inflated sense of responsibility for other people
- Excessively loyal to others even when it is not deserved
- The need to control others

Because these adults have suffered core damage as children, they never received the essential love and attention that is required to live a normal life and have normal relationships. The *inner child* of these individuals is severely damaged. We can define inner child as, "the place inside of ourselves where our most essential feelings live." For these adults to be happy and feel fulfilled requires that their inner child be awakened and given life.

"If you were emotionally abused or neglected as a child, there is likely still a child inside of you who needs to feel safe, who needs to be soothed, and who is aching to be cherished." — *Julie Levin*

Inner child healing is often done through a process known as re-parenting. Re-parenting is essentially the process of parenting yourself as an adult in order to reclaim the inner child that was lost due to the abuse, invalidation, or neglect suffered in childhood.

Any program or effort to re-parent ourselves must include the following elements:

- Making peace with the past and forgiving a parent who may have hurt us
- Absolute and unconditional self-love and self-acceptance
- Growing our self-esteem
- Putting our own needs above the needs of others
- Recognizing ourselves as lovable and worthy
- Doing what we believe to be right without seeking the approval of others

- Recognizing the difference between caring for others and "care-taking"
- Treating ourselves with kindness, sensitivity, and patience
- Honoring our own feelings, and
- Pursuing healthy relationships based on mutual love and respect where each partner gives and receives equally.

Some people are capable of recognizing their own deficits and can therefore begin the process of re-parenting themselves on their own incorporating the elements listed above.

Others will require the assistance of a mental health professional who deals with the issues of codependency and core childhood trauma. Re-parenting is a type of psychotherapy that aims to correct psychological behaviors that stem from neglect, trauma, abuse, or abandonment which occurred in childhood. Re-parenting often encourages a person to relive parent-induced trauma, with the therapist taking on the role of the parent, and responding appropriately to the patient.

Chapter 3: The role of shame in the developing personality

Any discussion of personality disorders and childhood trauma would not be complete without addressing the subject of shame. Shame has been called the most terrible emotion that a human being can experience. Shame has been referred to as *the hiding emotion* since shame sometimes makes us want to disappear. Shame experienced during childhood can be particularly damaging to one's long term emotional development. Childhood shame is sometimes referred to as *toxic shame.*

Shame is both a noun, as in *"Mike felt incredible shame whenever he was in the company of his grandfather,"* and a verb as in, *"Mike's grandfather routinely shamed him by calling him stupid and ugly."* Unlike other forms of discipline, shame takes aim directly at an individual's identity and their sense of self. Many adults routinely use shame as a form of discipline. However, while shaming a child may limit and even eliminate unwanted behavior, the damage done to the child's psyche and self-image can be devastating.

Shame is often confused with guilt, but the two are actually very different. Guilt tends to be short-lived and it normally reflects a feeling or regret about something that we have done or not done. A person may feel guilty about eating too much, staying up too late, drinking too much, forgetting a friend's birthday, or for not studying for an important exam. Guilt therefore can be a good thing since it helps us to correct our negative behavior.

Shame on the other hand is much different. First shame generally lasts much longer than guilt; childhood shame can endure for a lifetime. Shame is a much more painful emotion; it hurts us at a much deeper place than guilt. Shame can be so devastating that it actually has the ability to change not only our behavior but also our perception of ourselves. Childhood shame can be permanent and life altering.

Another very important distinction between guilt and shame is that guilt makes us feel bad or contrite about something that we have done or have not done. Shame on the other hand cuts much deeper; shame makes us feel bad about *who we are*. Shame touches us at a much more vulnerable place, and can cause permanent damage to our sense of *Self*.

When an adult punishes a child in the form of public yelling, name-calling, threats, insults, embarrassment, and humiliation the adult is shaming that child. That shame is stored in child's psyche and physiologically in an area of the brain known as the amygdala and becomes a part of what we call the *inner critic*. The impact of this can be devastating later in life.

"Shame restrains a child's self-expression: having felt the sting of an adult's negative judgment, the shamed child censors herself in order to escape being branded as "naughty" or "bad." Shame crushes children's natural exuberance, their curiosity, and their desire to do things by themselves." — Robin Grille

Childhood shame seems to be one of the factors that can lead to the development of adult emotional problems including anxiety, depression, eating disorders, ocd, and even personality disorders.

Dr. Brené Brown is a research professor at the University Of Houston Graduate College Of Social Work. Brown has a PhD in philosophy and is known primarily for her research on empathy, vulnerability, and shame. Speaking on the issue of shame Dr. Brené Brown has said:

"Shame works like the zoom lens on a camera. When we are feeling shame, the camera is zoomed in tight and all we see is our flawed selves, alone and struggling." — Dr. Brené Brown

The power of shame to damage and permanently alter a young child cannot be overstated. Childhood shame is the precursor to many negative behaviors in adults and even full-blown psychiatric disorders.

So just how powerful and far reaching is shame?

- Shame is anxiety
- Shame is depression
- Shame is emptiness
- Shame is social phobia
- Shame is panic
- Shame is low self-esteem
- Shame is self-loathing.
- Shame is loneliness.
- Shame is unworthiness

- Shame is the young boy with the stutter
- Shame is the girl with the promiscuous reputation
- Shame is the guy with the syringe injecting himself with heroin
- Shame is the man sitting in the bar drinking cheap whiskey long after everyone else has gone home.
- Shame is the young woman leaning over the toilet purging her last meal
- Shame is the compulsive hand washer.
- Shame is the hoarder
- Shame is self-injury and self-mutilation
- Shame is the binge eater
- Shame is the woman gazing in the mirror at her thin frail body searching for signs of fat
- Shame is the morbidly obese man who cannot get enough to eat
- Shame is the successful professional woman who continues to buy more than she needs long after she has maxed out her credit cards
- Shame is the perfectionist
- Shame is *I do not deserve*
- Shame is *I am not worthy*
- Shame is *I am not good enough*
- Shame is *I am not lovable*

Moreover, shame is the schizoid, the borderline, the narcissist, the histrionic, the avoidant, the dependent, and the codependent. If shame is so incredibly toxic, what if anything is its antidote? How does one overcome the powerful effects of shame? Overcoming shame and shame-based disorders is not easy; the truth is that most of those suffering with toxic shame will never be completely free of its effects.

However, thanks to the work of Dr. Brené Brown and others we know that there is hope for recovering from *shame* and shame based disorders. Any type of therapy or program whose objective is to reduce or to eliminate shame requires a motivated individual, with desire, insight, courage, determination, patience, and perhaps most important, the willingness to be *vulnerable.* The willingness to be vulnerable is essential to conquering shame. In addition exposing our shame to the empathetic ear of an attentive friend, family member, or mental health professional is essential.

"If we can share our story with someone who responds with empathy and understanding, shame can't survive." — *Brené Brown*

We must have the courage to take our shame out of the darkness and expose it to the light. We must be willing to share of stories of shame with another, preferably someone who can listen with understanding and empathy. As Dr. Brown points out, shame cannot survive when it is exposed to compassion and empathy. Therefore, if shame were the poison then compassion, understanding, and empathy are the antidotes.

Many shame-based disorders including those listed above can be healed through the process of talk therapy. To succeed the patient must have the courage to be vulnerable and give a voice to their deepest darkest shame. In addition, it is imperative that the therapist and the client establish a relationship based on trust and compassion. In time and with the right therapist our shame cannot survive. When shame encounters genuine empathy, more often than not empathy is victorious and shame melts away.

Chapter 4: Borderline Personality Disorder

Although first described in 1938 by American psychoanalyst Adolph Stern, borderline personality disorder was not officially recognized by the psychiatric community until 1980 with the release of the third revision of the Diagnostic and Statistical Manual of Psychiatry, DSM-III.

Why the term "borderline"? Psychoanalyst Adolf Stern coined the term *borderline* to describe a group of women he was treating in the 1930s and 1940s who seemed to exist on a precarious emotional border. The majority of the time they would exhibit primarily neurotic behavior, including depression, anxiety, and mood swings. However, under certain conditions they would go from being simply neurotic into a state of short-term *psychosis* (a loss of touch with reality). Abandonment or the expectation of separation from a loved one was often the cause of these brief psychotic episodes. It should be noted that these psychotic episodes were short-lived and for the vast majority of these borderline patients they exist primarily in a neurotic state.

For individuals with borderline personality psychotic breaks are rare. The majority tends to be high functioning and can easily blend in with any crowd. In fact, those with BPD are sometimes referred to as *chameleons*, because of their ability to blend and to become whoever they need to be in a given situation or environment.

BPD (Borderline personality disorder) is the most well-known and frequently diagnosed of the personality disorders. It is believed to affect approximately six percent of the adult population (that is nearly 10 million American adults) and although it was once considered largely a female disorder, it is now believed to affect men and women in equal numbers. Although there remains considerable controversy over the exact cause of borderline personality disorder, it would appear that it is neither all biological nor all parenting but a combination of several factors including the temperament or disposition of the child.

The term *biopsychosocial* refers to a condition whose origin is a combination of biological, psychological, and social factors. Borderline personality, like other personality disorders, is believed to be the result of biopsychosocial factors, meaning that it has its origin partially in the genes of a parent, (mother or father), in the child's environment (the manner in which the child was parented), and in the psychology of the child (the child's temperament and disposition).

In addition to the genetic and biological component, which comes from either the mother or the father, borderline personality disorder appears to have its roots in the child's early relationship with the mother and the all-important bonding process that occurs between an infant and a mother in the first year of life commonly referred to as *attunement*.

Attunement can be described as the manner in which a mother and an infant interact and respond to one another. An attentive emotionally available mother is able to recognize the subtle physical and emotional needs of her infant. The process of attunement is largely non-verbal and is a reciprocal process between a mother and a child. When the process is carried out effectively, it is often described as a dance or *"the dance of attunement."* Attunement sets the stage for what is referred to in psychology as *infant attachment.*

"When parents tune in to and respond to their children's needs and are a dependable source of comfort, those children learn how to manage their own feeling and behaviors. These secure attachments to their mothers and fathers provide these children with a base from which they can thrive." — Sophie Moullin

A successful attunement process will normally lead to what is known as a *secure attachment* whereby a child will go on to have healthy adult relationships. However, if the attunement process is thwarted either because of an inattentive, depressed, or substance-abusing mother the child risks becoming *insecurely attached.* Fortunately, 60% of American infants form secure attachments with their mothers. However, another 40% do not and of those, 15% have what is referred to as a *fearful avoidant attachment.* Individuals with a fearful avoidant attachment style feel unworthy and untrusting and have a difficult time trusting others. Fearful avoidant attachment puts an individual at a higher risk for developing a personality disorder.

According to the 4th Edition of the Psychiatric DSM an individual must have at least five of the following nine symptoms in order to qualify for a diagnosis of BPD:

1. **Frantic efforts to avoid real or imagined abandonment**

2. **A pattern of unstable and intense interpersonal relationships** characterized by alternating between extremes of idealization and devaluation

3. **Identity disturbance**, such as a significant and persistent unstable self-image or sense of self

4. **Impulsivity** in at least two areas that are potentially self-damaging (e.g., spending, sex, substance abuse, reckless driving, binge eating)

5. **Recurrent suicidal behavior**, gestures, or threats, or self-mutilating behavior

6. **Emotional instability** due to significant reactivity of mood (e.g., intense episodic dysphoria, irritability, or anxiety usually lasting a few hours and only rarely more than a few days)

7. **Chronic feelings of emptiness**

8. **Inappropriate, intense anger** or difficulty controlling anger (e.g., frequent displays of temper, constant anger, recurrent physical fights)

9. **Transient, stress-related paranoid thoughts** or severe dissociative symptoms

Prominent Symptoms of BPD explained:

1. **Fear of abandonment:** People with borderline personality disorder have a fear of being abandoned, rejected, or left alone. This is the most prominent symptom of borderline personality disorder. The deepest fear of people with BPD is being left alone. Even perceived rejection or the expectation of being rejected can drive a person with BPD into panic, depression, rage, and, in the worst cases, a *psychotic* state.

2. **Splitting:** This is sometimes referred to as *black and white or dichotomous thinking*. People who suffer with BPD have arrested emotional development that does not allow them to see grays or nuance. They view themselves and others as being either all good or all bad. They have difficulty with the concept that good people can sometimes do bad things. A person with BPD may say, *"I love you"* one day and *"I hate you"* the next.

3. **Rage:** This is sometimes referred to as *inappropriate anger.* Rage is essentially anger out of proportion. People with BPD are subject to sudden outbursts of intense anger or rage. This may or may not include physical violence. Because they tend to be highly sensitive to real or perceived criticism, they react in a very emotional way when their expectations of others are not met.

4. **Feelings of emptiness:** The feeling is associated with loneliness and neediness. Those with BPD use words such as *"hollowness"* to describe the experience.

5. **Mood instability:** Unlike bipolar disorder where a person undergoes mood changes over regular and predictable intervals, those with BPD will experience dramatic mood swings that occur over the course of a single day or even within hours. These can include feelings of depression, anxiety, anger, irritation, and even transient psychosis.

6. **Impulsive behavior:** People with BPD are incredibly impulsive and as a result often act in a reckless manner. This impulsive behavior may come in the form of substance abuse, binge eating, reckless driving, excessive spending, promiscuous sex, and gambling, etc.

7. **Unstable relationships:** Those with BPD have a difficult time maintaining relationships with friends, romantic partners, and even family members. Their relationships tend to be very emotional, turbulent, and chaotic. A person with BPD will often over idealize (exaggerate a person's positives) then devalue (exaggerate a person's negatives) the people in their life.

8. **Poor self-image**: People with borderline personality often struggle with feelings of insecurity, low self-esteem, poor self-image, and something referred to as *identity*

confusion. It is not unusual for someone with BPD not to really know *who they are.* This is a difficult thing to explain but it goes back to their first year of life and a disruption in the all-important maternal/infant attunement process.

9. **Substance abuse:** The majority of people with BPD will abuse alcohol or other substances at some point in their lifetime and in some cases for many years.

The following are the typical thoughts of someone with BPD:

- *I cannot trust anyone.*
- *Please do not leave me.*
- *I need for you to love me.*
- *No one will ever love me.*
- *Everyone is going to leave me.*
- *I need someone to take care of me.*
- *I am a bad person.*
- *I cannot cope on my own; I need someone to rely on.*

While there is no single cure for borderline personality disorder, people do improve. When it comes to the symptoms of borderline, many of the most severe ones tend to diminish, as one ages. In addition, there are medications to treat the symptoms that accompany BPD such as anxiety, depression, and mood swings.

Cognitive behavioral therapy has shown to be effective in treating BPD and in particular, a newer form of therapy known as *Dialectic Behavioral Therapy* developed in 1993 by Marsha Lineman. DBT teaches patients with borderline personality a number of important skills including mindfulness, distress tolerance, interpersonal effectiveness, and emotional regulation.

Examples of female movie/film characters with BPD:

- Jessica Walter as Evelyn Draper, Play Misty for Me, 1971
- Glenn Close as Alexandra "Alex" Forrest, Fatal Attraction, 1987
- Jessica Lange as Frances Farmer, Frances, 1982
- Alicia Silverstone as Adrian Forrester, The Crush, 1993
- Rosamund Pike as Amy Elliott Dunne, Gone Girl, 2014

Chapter 5: Understanding the Nine Symptoms of BPD

They are nine clinical symptoms listed in the Diagnostic and Statistical Manual of Psychiatry 4th edition for BPD. A person need only have five of the nine in order to receive a diagnosis of BPD. That means that there are actually 256 possible combinations of symptoms, which makes each borderline patient unique.

The following are the nine clinical symptoms of BPD along with a brief explanation of each.

1. **Fear of abandonment:** This is the hallmark symptom of this disorder. Those with borderline personality believe that the people in their life are going to abandon or reject them. They will often anticipate being abandoned or they will misinterpret the actions of a spouse, or other loved one as rejection or desertion. The fear of being abandoned or "left alone" is considered the core symptom of borderline personality disorder. Anticipation of a separation or breakup can send a person with into panic, rage, or even *transient psychosis*.

2. **Unstable intense relationships:** Because they were insecurely attached as infants and often abused or neglected as children, people with borderline personality disorder are often very dependent and anxious when it comes to romantic relationships. They have a difficult time maintaining long-term stable relationships. More often than not, it is the borderlines own self-defeating

behaviors that will result in these short-lived stormy relationships.

3. **Identity disturbance:** People with borderline personality disorder often *"do not know who they are."* Those with this disorder sometimes do not feel like the same person from day to day. They are sometimes described as chameleons in that they can become whomever they need to be to blend in with those around them. The reason for this is not entirely clear but as infants, they developed insecure attachments with their mothers or primary caregivers. A secure infant mother attachment is critical to developing a stable sense of self. The borderline's personality has never become fully integrated into *a whole personality.*

4. **Impulsivity and recklessness:** The opposite of being impulsive is to be reflective and although those with BPD can also be reflective, they are often quite impulsive. People with borderline personality will often engage in activities for the emotional high or short-term relief from their negative feelings. These activities include excessive spending, binge eating, reckless driving and speeding, substance abuse, and promiscuous sex.

5. **Suicidal thoughts or gestures:** Self-injury (cutting or burning) is common among people with borderline personality disorder. Nearly everyone who suffers with this disorder contemplates suicide at some point. It is estimated that as many as 8 out of 10 people suffering

with BPD will attempt suicide, and one in 10 will eventually succeed. BPD has one of the highest mortality rates of any mental health disorder.

6. **Emotional instability:** People with borderline personality experience dramatic mood swings in reaction to people and situations. Unlike those with bipolar disorder these moods swings can occur many times throughout a single day. They can include periods of sadness, irritability, anxiety, panic, and anger. One moment they may be cheerful and optimistic, then after a negative experience, they will suddenly become angry and depressed.

7. **Chronic feelings of emptiness:** People with borderline personality disorder often feel empty inside. It is described as a kind of *visceral hollowness* felt in the abdomen. It is more than just depression or boredom but more like a feeling of emotional deprivation. Again, the root cause is not completely understood.

8. **Explosive anger:** People with borderline personality disorder often experience periods of intense anger. This anger is brought on by a perceived criticism, rejection, or abandonment. Rage can be thought of as anger, which is out of proportion for a given situation.

9. **Stress-related paranoid thoughts:** Under periods of extreme stress, a person with borderline personality

disorder can experience what is known as a *dissociative episode.* Unlike the paranoia experienced with other psychiatric disorders, the dissociative episode tends to be brief. This particular symptom sets borderline apart from all other personality disorders in that the individual can drift into a kind of psychotic state whereby they can temporarily "lose touch with reality."

Chapter 6: Other behaviors associated with BPD

In addition to the nine clinical symptoms of BPD, there are a host of other behaviors that are common among those with BPD. The following are additional symptoms and behaviors associated with BPD. These are not the clinical symptoms and this is by no means a complete list of behaviors.

- Anxiety
- Depression
- Mood swings
- Panic
- Fear of rejection
- Feelings of insecurity
- Stalking
- Feelings of desperation
- Grandiosity
- Egocentrism
- Narcissism
- Jealousy
- Projection
- Lying and manipulation
- Projection
- Anger and rage
- Black and white or dichotomous thinking
- Feelings of emptiness
- Fear of being alone. (Monophobia)
- Sexual promiscuity
- Sexual addiction

- Fear of intimacy
- Relationship anxiety
- Substance abuse (alcohol and drugs)
- Highly sensitive temperament
- Self-injury (cutting, burning, etc.)
- Poor self-image (low self-esteem)
- Self-loathing (hatred of oneself)
- Body image issues or body dysmorphia
- Eating disorders; bulimia, anorexia, binge eating
- Preoccupation with youth and beauty
- Paranoia and suspiciousness
- Depersonalization
- Derealization
- Inability to accept blame

These not a complete list of *borderline behaviors,* nor are these behaviors exclusive to those with BPD. However, these behaviors, in addition, to the nine clinical symptoms are common in many who suffer with borderline personality disorder.

Chapter 7: Recognizing BPD in a woman you are dating.

The women who qualify for a diagnosis of BPD tend to be very sweet and romantic. They are also known for their heightened sensitivity. For many men these qualities make them so appealing. They often make great friends and can be very exciting women to date.

However, if a man's intention is to have a long-term relationship with this woman, he may be in for a surprise. A man who has never dated a borderline woman will soon find that she is unlike any woman he has ever met.

In relationships, borderline women present a unique challenge. Moreover, while a man should certainly not discount this woman as a partner or spouse, it is helpful to understand how, and why she behaves in the manner she does.

Here are TEN signs that the woman you are dating may have BPD:

1. She makes you feel incredibly special and says things to you that no woman has ever said. This can be a very powerful experience for a man and depending on how much dating experience a man has had; one could easily believe this is the woman of his dreams. Borderline woman are known to engage in something called *idealization.* In psychology idealization is a mental process whereby an individual concentrates on and

emphasizes someone's positive traits, and pays no attention to the negative ones. Idealization is quite common and necessary in children with regard to their parents, but in adults, it can be unhealthy.

2. She quickly begins using the word *"love,"* often within the first few dates. This can be incredibly captivating to a man and it may even sound genuine. However, as most people know, love does not happen in a matter of days or weeks. Obviously, this is not real love. So what is it? When a borderline woman, or a borderline man for that matter, declares their love, they are essentially saying that, *"they need or want for you to love them."*

3. She makes her ex-husband or ex-boyfriend out to be a bad person or even abusive. She is most likely exaggerating. In truth, any man who was married to or in a relationship with this woman would certainly have good reasons for being frustrated, confused, and even hurt due to the challenges associated with being in a relationship with her.

4. She buys you very nice, even expensive gifts, very early in the relationship.

5. She talks about how her ex cheated on her. Maybe he did and maybe he did not, but it is just as likely that she cheated on him. Borderline woman are more likely than the average woman to cheat in relationships. The

reasons for this are complicated and a borderline woman can often justify her own cheating.

6. She had sex with you on the first or the second date. This is often an attempt to grab a man's attention and to secure his love.

7. She drinks to excess and perhaps uses drugs. Alcohol, prescription drugs, and recreational drugs are one of the quickest and most efficient ways for those with BPD to soothe their deep emotional pain and anxiety.

8. She gets very jealous when you talk about other women, even female friends. Borderline women are very insecure and they view other women as a threat. They often develop something called *delusional jealousy*, which will cause them to imagine that their partner is being unfaithful.

9. She has a very difficult time with compliments. One of the underlying issues with BPD is a sense of being defective, unworthy, and unlovable. Women with BPD generally have low self-esteem, which borders on *self-loathing*. As a result, they will often doubt and question the sincerity of compliments.

10. She has problems accepting blame or apologizing. This is certainly not true of all women with BPD, but it is for many. The willingness to apologize or to accept blame is

a trait that is common to both narcissists and borderlines. The reasons for this are complicated.

The dating pool, including online dating sites, is full of women with borderline traits and BPD and a man should not discount these women for a relationship or even as a potential spouse. These women are generally sensitive, romantic, and caring. However, they do present a man with unique challenges and not every man will be capable or willing to deal with the challenge of being involved with a woman who suffers with BPD.

Chapter 8: Borderline Personality in Males

Borderline personality disorder in men or MBPD (Male Borderline Personality Disorder) has only recently begun to receive serious attention from the psychiatric community. There had long been a bias among therapists that BPD was predominantly or even exclusively a female disorder. As a result, men with borderline symptoms would often be misdiagnosed with things such as antisocial personality disorder, substance abuse disorders, PTSD, or even bipolar disorder.

It has been referred to by some as the *Casanova disorder,* and until recently, it was one of psychiatry's best-kept secrets. There may be several reasons for this. Perhaps it is because these behaviors in males, which are nearly identical to those in women, are considered more acceptable in men. In addition, men are much less likely than women to seek treatment for their mental and emotional problems.

The disorder has a strong link to early childhood and the mother/son relationship. As an adult, the male borderline is believed to be searching for the female nurturing and affection that he never received as a boy. This is not to negate the biological component that also is believed to play a role in the development of this disorder.

"A hallmark trait of BPD, the inability to manage inner feelings, is just as present in the male, but it often manifests as spousal abuse or other violent acts rather than the self-directed anger more often

seen in the female borderline" — *Rex Cowdry, MD*

Many men, who are incarcerated in our nation's prisons, in addition to qualifying for a diagnosis of antisocial personality disorder, would also meet the requirements for BPD or MBPD.

Prominent symptoms of MBPD:

1. **Abandonment fears:** This is the hallmark feature of this disorder and it is equally present in both men and women. Borderline men are just as terrified of abandonment as women and in relationships they tend to be clingy and needy.

2. **Grandiose/narcissistic:** Borderline men tend to be boastful and egocentric. They are grandiose in the way they think and talk about themselves. They will brag, exaggerate, and lie about their accomplishments and their abilities. In reality, this is merely an attempt to compensate for a fragile ego.

3. **Overly jealous:** Borderline men are very insecure despite their sometimes-seeming confidence. In relationships, they will react with hostility and jealousy around other males. Borderline men are overly possessive and exhibit *inappropriate jealousy.*

4. **Sensitive and romantic:** Men with BPD tend to be more sensitive and romantic than the average guy. This is one of the qualities that women initially find most appealing about them.

5. **Short-lived intense relationships:** Men with BPD have a difficult time forming long-lasting romantic relationships due to fears of intimacy and commitment. As a result, they tend to have many short-term volatile relationships. As soon as one relationship ends, the male borderline will often begin pursuing a new one.

6. **Mood swings:** Like women, men with BPD experience frequent mood swings. He can go from being narcissistic and egotistical to being depressed, insecure, and back to self-confident within a very short period.

7. **Sex addiction:** Borderline men have a very difficult time with genuine intimacy. They will often confuse intimacy and sex. Some borderline men are genuinely addicted to sex and pornography.

8. **Substance abuse:** Like women, borderline men also tend to abuse alcohol and/or drugs. Because of their inability to self-soothe or deal with their emotional pain in healthy ways, drugs and alcohol are quick and easy escapes for them.

9. **Sensitive to criticism:** Borderline men are incredibly thin skinned and hypersensitive to real or perceived criticism or negative remarks. Criticism can send them into a state of rage, which can often turn to physical violence.

10. **Suspicious and untrusting:** Because their internal dialogue is that, *they are unworthy and unlovable,* borderline men tend to be very jealous in relationships. No matter how much they are reassured, they are simply incapable of trusting. They will often test women, sometimes repeatedly, in an attempt to reassure themselves.

11. **Reckless:** Borderline men engage is risky, impulsive, and reckless behavior. This includes things such as reckless driving, drinking, drug use, promiscuous sex, gambling, overspending, etc.

12. **Low self-esteem:** *At* the heart of this disorder is a man who feels incredibly insecure and inadequate. This is often the result of being the product of an emotionally unavailable mother or caregiver who never met his boyhood needs for affection and love.

13. **Intense anger/rage:** Anger is common to all borderlines, and it is often extreme and *out of proportion* for the situation. Real or perceived slights, criticisms, or fear of being left alone are some of the things that can cause this

male to go off the deep end. Physical violence is much more common in the male borderline.

14. **Suicidal thoughts:** Borderline men often engage in suicidal thoughts or ideation. Half of all borderlines attempt suicide at least once, and ten percent will go on to complete suicide.

"Borderline men frequently engage in addictive, sexually compulsive behaviors, including regularly hiring prostitutes, having serial affairs, going to strip clubs, obsessively viewing pornography, engaging in voyeurism or exhibitionism, and compulsive masturbation. Some borderline men even use high-risk sex as a form of self-harm." — Mary Gay, PhD.

There is currently no cure for borderline personality disorder. However, with the proper treatment and time, patients can make significant improvements. Many of the symptoms such as anxiety, depression, and mood swings can be managed with medication. Talk therapy and in particular, a form of therapy developed in the 90s called DBT or Dialectical Behavioral Therapy, has been found to be particularly helpful.

Men who suffer with borderline personality disorder are not bad people and they are not out to hurt women. In truth, they are simply looking for love and acceptance like most people. However, BPD is a potentially serious psychiatric disorder that requires the treatment of a mental health professional.

Examples of male movie/film characters with BPD:

- Mark Wahlberg as David McCall, Fear, 1996
- Rob Lowe as Alex, Bad Influence, 1990
- William Baldwin as Zeke Hawkins, Sliver, 1993
- Michael Douglas as Steven Taylor, A Perfect Murder, 1998
- Robert De Niro as Jake La Motta, Raging Bull, 1980

Chapter 9: Ten signs that you're dating a man with BPD

For many years, we have thought of borderline personality disorder as being a female disorder. However, we now know that there may be just as male borderlines in the dating pool as female. While this man should not be ruled out for a long–term relationship, a woman should be aware that she is getting involved with an emotionally unhealthy man with major *"mommy issues."*

Although borderline men can seem quite normal at first, in time a woman will discover that a relationship with this male is anything but normal.

"Usually adult males who are unable to make emotional connections with the women they choose to be intimate with are frozen in time; unable to allow themselves to love for fear that the loved one will abandon them. If the first woman they passionately loved, the mother, was not true to her bond of love, then how can they trust that their partner will be true to love. Often in their adult relationships, these men act out repeatedly to test their partner's love." — Gloria Jean Watkins

Here are TEN signs that you may be dating a man with BPD:

1. **He comes on very strong and he is romantic:** Borderline men tend to be very sensitive and romantic. In a sense, they are addicted to the notion of romance and love. Initially this can be one of the more alluring qualities of these men. You may even

think, "this guy sounds too good to be true." (And, just as with all things that sound too good to be true, so is the male borderline.)

2. **Quick to declare his love**: A borderline man will sometimes profess his love on a first or second date. In truth, borderline men either have a distorted idea of love, or simply do not know what real love is. It is not that they are trying to be deceitful; it is just that their early template of love is a distorted one.

3. **Substance abuse issues:** This includes alcohol, and drugs like cocaine, marijuana, and all types of pills. Chemical addiction among borderline men is very common. This male is essentially self-medicating himself in order to soothe his deep emotional pain and his feelings of being unlovable.

4. **Excessive jealousy:** Borderline men are very insecure despite their apparent confidence. In relationships, they will react with anger and jealousy around other males. Borderline men are possessive and exhibit *inappropriate jealousy*, meaning they will even become jealous over a woman's male friends.

5. **Grandiose:** Borderline men tend to be boastful and egotistical. They are grandiose in the way they think and talk about themselves. They will brag, exaggerate, and lie about their accomplishments and

their abilities. In reality, this is merely an attempt to compensate for a fragile ego.

6. **Great lovers:** Borderline men tend to be hypersexual can even be genuine sexual addicts. Women often describe them as fantastic lovers and very giving in the bedroom. Since borderline men are generally incapable of true intimacy they will often use sex as a replacement for intimacy or love. In addition, a borderline man will use sex as a way of winning or securing a woman.

7. **The suggestion of a breakup sends him off** *the deep end***:** At the heart of BPD is the issue of abandonment. The male was likely abandoned by an absent or ineffective mother at an early age. As a result, he has also developed feelings of *misogyny*. Any indication of a breakup, whether real or perceived, will cause a dramatic reaction in this male. It may come in the form of fear, rage, or great sadness. It is not unheard of for someone with BPD to preemptively end a relationship if he feels that a breakup is imminent.

8. **Impulsive and reckless:** Impulsive behavior is another hallmark feature of BPD. This may come in the form of excessive gambling, promiscuous and unprotected sex, reckless driving, excessive spending, driving while intoxicated, and frequent drinking or

drug use.

9. **Bad temper:** The male borderline, like the female, has a bad temper. Slights, real or imagined, will bring on this man's anger. His anger tends to be extreme and out of proportion for the situation. It is not uncommon for borderline men to turn physically violent.

10. **Mood instability**: Affective instability or mood swings are a classic symptom of borderline personality. This man's moods can go up and down many times in a single day. His mood swings are both a result of his temperament and neurology and a reaction to situational factors.

Men who suffer with BPD are not bad people and they are not out to hurt women. In truth, they are simply looking for love and acceptance like everyone else. However, BPD is a serious psychiatric disorder that requires long-term treatment with a mental health professional. A woman who gets involved with this man cannot fix or rescue him with kindness, compassion, or love. The only way a man like this can improve is on his own terms and in his own time. In addition to the help of a mental health professional, that requires insight, courage, and desire.

Chapter 10:   Coping strategies for those with BPD

The following are some non-pharmaceutical coping strategies or techniques that can be particularly helpful to those who suffer with BPD.

1. **Practice benign interpretation:** For any given event or situation there are an infinite number of possible interpretations. However, people with BPD have a tendency to assume the worst and choose the interpretation that reflects most negatively on them. For example if someone is late for a meeting, the BP would likely assume that, "the person isn't coming," or "they never intended to show up in the first place." Benign interpretation means NOT assuming the worst. It means entertaining positive healthy thoughts like "the person is running late," or "the person got stuck in traffic." In the vast majority of cases, the benign explanation will be much closer to the actual explanation.

2. **Feelings are not facts:** Remember just because we feel something does not make it true. We cannot automatically assume that what we are feeling is based on what is actually happening. Get more information before drawing a conclusion. It may sound counterintuitive but for some people, particularly the BP, they should always NOT always trust their instincts. (For example, *"I feel like everyone hates me"*. Based on

what?)

3. **Avoid alcohol**: For the borderline personality, drinking alcohol can be like throwing gasoline on a fire. All of the worst feelings and behaviors can come to the surface. Alcohol has a way of getting the borderline into trouble and often results in feelings of regret and shame. Unfortunately, alcohol is often the self-medication of choice for the BP.

4. **Do go to bed angry:** The old adage of *never go to bed angry* does not apply to the borderline. When someone with borderline personality gets upset or angry they should resist the temptation to act on their anger and instead sleep on it. In the majority of cases, the anger will be gone the following day and oftentimes the borderline will no longer remember or be as troubled by what occurred the previous day.

5. **Exercise**: Exercise is the answer for so many people and the BP is no exception. In addition to the beneficial effects on the body, exercise is a great way to dissipate stress and anger. It is also a very good way of distracting one's obsessive thoughts.

6. **Challenge negative thoughts:** People who suffer with BPD have an extremely harsh internal dialogue, which is disproportionally negative in thoughts and messages. In the same way that feelings are not facts, thoughts are not

facts either. Just because one thinks, something does not make it so. (For example, *"I don't think I can give this speech!"* Based on what?)

7. **Take a deep breath:** Sometimes just taking a deep breath and waiting thirty seconds or a minute to respond to a situation can make all the difference in terms of reacting appropriately. This is true for many people but it is particularly true for the BP. People with BP tend to be hypersensitive and impulsive. Taking that deep breath and having that extra time to focus and think before reacting can result in a response that is not only more composed but also more accurate.

Chapter 11: Relationship Anxiety

People who suffer with relationship anxiety have a difficult time sustaining long-term romantic relationships. Unlike those who have chosen to remain single, the majority of people with relationship anxiety would prefer to be in a committed relationship. However, the stress and anxiety they experience while in a relationship is too overwhelming for them to handle. As a result, their romantic relationships are either short-lived or non-existent.

"There are two basic motivating forces: fear and love. When we are afraid, we pull back from life. When we are in love, we open to all that life has to offer with passion, excitement, and acceptance. We need to learn to love ourselves first, in all our glory and our imperfections. If we cannot love ourselves, we cannot fully open to our ability to love others or our potential to create. Evolution and all hopes for a better world rest in the fearlessness and open-hearted vision of people who embrace life." — John Lennon

Relationship anxiety is not formally recognized as a psychiatric disorder. Therefore, the term cannot be found in the Diagnostic and Statistical Manual. In its mildest form, it is sometimes referred to as being *love shy.* At its most severe is can manifest as *borderline personality disorder.* It is impossible to know how many people suffer with this condition but it is believed to affect men and women in equal numbers.

People with relationship anxiety tend to exhibit common behaviors, which include:

- Excessive or inappropriate jealousy
- Being overly needy or clingy
- Inability to trust
- Being aloof and disinterested
- A constant need for reassurance from their partner
- Testing their partner
- "Push pull" behavior (A pattern of disrupting and reestablishing closeness in a relationship without appropriate cause or reason
- Emotional volatility or impulsivity

There are a number of factors that make one more likely to develop relationship anxiety. The most common are:

- Negative early dating experiences going back to adolescence
- Insecure attachment with a mother or primary caregiver during infancy (anxious attachment, avoidant attachment, or fearful attachment)
- An abusive or neglectful childhood
- Low self-esteem
- Fear of intimacy (anxiety over allowing oneself to be emotionally vulnerable)
- Fear of rejection

In addition, people with relationship anxiety are more likely to suffer with other problems including anxiety, depression, social anxiety, alcoholism or other substance abuse problems.

The issues that contribute to relationship anxiety do not generally go away on their own. Therefore, relationship anxiety tends to be a chronic lifelong condition. If an individual fails to address it then it is likely they will remain forever-single going from one short-term relationship to the next or never getting into relationships at all.

No matter what the specific cause of one's relationship anxiety, there appears to be a common theme that dominates the internal dialogue of these individuals, and that is the conscious or unconscious belief that they are somehow *unworthy, defective, or unlovable*. Moreover, until the individual is willing to confront and acknowledge the absurdity and untruthfulness of those feelings then they will continue to struggle in their romantic relationships.

There is no single cure for relationship anxiety; however, individuals can make tremendous progress through talk therapy with a qualified sympathetic mental health professional. Medications that treat anxiety and depression can also be helpful.

Therefore, while there is no quick fix for this condition there is hope for those who suffer with relationship anxiety. Like so many conditions that plague the human psyche the answer, at least in part, lies in unconditional self-acceptance and love.

Chapter 12: Narcissistic Personality Disorder

Narcissism has become one of the most overused labels in American culture. Narcissism in its simplest form can be defined as, *love of oneself.* A certain amount of narcissism is healthy and necessary in all of us. However, like all human traits, narcissism exists on a broad continuum and in its extreme form; it can cause personal distress as well as social and occupational impairment.

"It is an absolute human certainty that no one can know his own beauty or perceive a sense of his own worth until it has been reflected back to him in the mirror of another loving, caring human being." — John Joseph Powell

To be narcissistic is much different that being a clinical narcissist. Someone who is narcissistic is self–absorbed, egotistical, arrogant, boastful, etc. To be a narcissist in the truest sense is very different. Clinical narcissism or NPD is a lifelong psychiatric disorder with no effective treatments and no cure.

Narcissism gets its name from the character in Greek mythology, *Narcissus*, who caught a glimpse of his reflection in a pond and became so enamored with himself (his reflection) that he eventually fell into the water and drowned. The metaphor of the reflecting pond is an appropriate one. Narcissus was not in love with himself, he was in love and captivated with his reflection. There is a huge difference between the two. If someone genuinely loves himself, then he loves himself regardless of the circumstances. His love is not dependent on anything or anyone. The narcissist does not love his true self; he rather loves his reflected or false self as seen through the eyes of others.

The irony of narcissism is that despite the definition the narcissist is actually quite insecure and *thin-skinned*. We may even go so far as to say that the narcissist suffers with a kind of self-loathing. At the heart of the narcissist is an incredibly fragile ego that has gone to incredible lengths to protect itself.

"The mythological Narcissus rejected the advances of the nymph Echo and was punished by the goddess Nemesis. He was consigned to pine away as he fell in love with his own reflection - exactly as Echo had pined away for him. How appropriate. Narcissists are punished by echoes and reflections of their problematic personalities up to this very day. Narcissists are said to be in love with themselves. But this is a fallacy. Narcissus is not in love with himself. He is in love with his reflection. There is a major difference between one's True Self and reflected-self." — *Sam Vaknin*

NPD or narcissistic personality disorder is the full-blown psychiatric disorder whereby an individual is grandiose, requires admiration, devalues others, has difficulty accepting blame, and is psychologically incapable of empathizing with the needs and the feelings of others.

While the precise cause of NPD is not completely understood, it is believed to be the result of both genetics and one's early childhood environment and experiences. At one time, NPD was believed to be caused by parents who excessively praised or pampered the child. However, it is now generally believed to be the result of childhood marked by neglect, emotional invalidation, and an insecure infant mother attachment.

The most recent estimates put the prevalence rate for narcissistic personality disorder at around six percent of the adult population. It is believed to be more common in men than in women although the reasons for this are not clear.

According to the 4th Edition of the Diagnostic and Statistical Manual of psychiatry, the following are the nine symptoms of NPD. An individual need on have five to meet the diagnosis:

1. Grandiosity or an exaggerated sense of one's own abilities and achievements
2. Persistent fantasies about attaining success and power
3. The belief that one is unique or "special," and should only associate with other people of the same status
4. The excessive need for attention, affirmation, and praise
5. A sense of entitlement and expectation of special treatment
6. Exploiting other people for personal gain

7. Feeling envious of others, or believing that others are envious of you
8. A lack of empathy for the needs and feelings of others
9. Arrogance

Typical thoughts of someone suffering with NPD:

- *I do not have to abide by the rules that apply to others.*
- *It is important to get recognition, praise, and admiration.*
- *If others do not respect my status, they should be punished.*
- *Other people should recognize how special I am.*
- *People have no right to criticize me.*
- *No one's needs should interfere with my own.*
- *Only people as brilliant as I am understand me.*

Narcissism is very different from being confident or thinking highly of oneself. People who are confident in a healthy way do not need to devalue or ridicule others in order to feel good about themselves. Narcissists are not the most agreeable people to be around and in some cases they can cause significant emotional damage to others, particularly family members.

People with NPD come across as conceited, boastful, and pretentious. They will often monopolize conversations. They may belittle or even ridicule people they perceive as inferior. They are grandiose and have a sense of entitlement. In addition, when they do not receive the special treatment to which they feel entitled, they may become very impatient or angry.

However, the two most disturbing traits of NPD is the narcissist's *inability to accept blame* and his *absence of genuine empathy*. For the narcissist to admit to being wrong, accepting blame, or offer a genuine apology would result in a significant and painful blow to his fragile ego and to his sense of self. Therefore, it is very rare for someone with NPD to say, *"It was my fault, I am sorry."*

In addition to this, the narcissist is incapable of empathizing with the feelings and the needs of others. It is these two toxic characteristics, the *lack of empathy and the projection of blame*, which cause the most damage to the people around the narcissist and to family members in particular.

A discussion of NPD would not be complete without addressing the toxic behaviors or for the *narcissist ego coping mechanisms* that are common in narcissists. Narcissists will often engage in destructive behavior that can cause significant distress and emotional harm to their friends and family members. These behaviors' include:

1. **Lying:** Whether it is being untruthful or lying by omission, this is a favorite tactic of the narcissist. Rather than the all-painful process of accepting blame, the narcissist will lie to spare his fragile ego.

2. **Gaslighting**: A form of emotional abuse whereby the narcissists will deny facts, events, and information causing the victim to question and doubt themselves. If done over a prolonged period it can cause an individual

to even question their sanity.

3. **Diversion:** A tactic used by the narcissist whereby he avoids responding to a direct question and tries to steer the conversation in a different direction.

4. **Triangulation:** A tactic whereby the narcissist will avoid one party and seek out a third party in order to garner support or an ally thereby further isolating the victim.

5. **Silent Treatment:** A form of emotional abuse whereby the narcissist will remain silent rather than respond to the needs or requests of the victim.

6. **Projection:** A tactic whereby the narcissist will place his own unacceptable thoughts or behavior onto the victim.

Does the narcissist intentionally set out to hurt others? Some would say "yes" while others would say "no." Again, we can go back to the introduction to this book and the subject of symptoms and behaviors as a means to satisfy one's deepest unmet needs. Using this explanation the narcissist is merely doing whatever he can to get what he so desperately needs or to protect his fragile sense of self.

Unfortunately, all too often, the price for this is the distress and emotional suffering of those associated with the narcissist, and all too often, this is the spouse and the children.

"Half the harm that is done in this world is due to people who want to feel important. They do not mean to do harm; but the harm does not interest them. Or they do not see it, or they justify it because they are absorbed in the endless struggle to think well of themselves." — *T.S. Eliot*

Surprisingly, the narcissist and the borderline have much in common in terms of their origin and their behaviors. Both of these disorders are considered disorders of the *Self*, meaning the identity or core of these individuals is incomplete and impaired. As a result, they both have what can be referred to as *arrested emotional development*. Many of the behaviors in these individuals including their egocentrism, their deficits in empathy, and their rage are behaviors we normally associate with young children. Therefore, we can say that both the n*arcissist* and the b*orderline* are still trapped in a kind of *perpetual childhood.*

Other similarities between the two include *fear of being abandoned,* however for slightly different reasons. While the borderline cannot tolerate the feeling of aloneness, the narcissist cannot thrive for very long without someone to admire him and feed his need for *narcissistic supply.* In addition, both of these personalities have a difficult time *accepting blame* and they both tend to be thin skinned and will often *rage* when slighted or criticized.

Narcissistic personality disorder is perhaps the most treatment resistant of all the personality disorders. Due to the very nature of this disorder and the narcissist's false belief that he is somehow *perfect* a narcissist will rarely seek professional help in the way of therapy.

If a narcissist does find himself in therapy, he will often insist that it is the people in his life that are the source of his distress since it is so incredibly difficult for him to take responsibility for his behavior or accept the idea that he is in any way imperfect.

Examples of movie/film characters with Narcissistic personality disorder include:

- Faye Dunaway as Joan Crawford, Mommie Dearest, 1981
- Michael Douglas as Gordon Gekko, Wall Street 1987
- Christian Bale as Patrick Bateman, American Psycho, 2000
- Will Ferrell as Ron Burgundy, Anchorman: The Legend of Ron Burgundy, 2004
- Tom Cruise as Charlie Babbitt, Rain Man, 1988s

Chapter 13: Twenty signs that you may be dating a narcissist

If the borderline woman presents a unique challenge for the single man, then for the single woman it is the narcissist male. The data suggests that clinical narcissism is more common in males, although there may be a cultural/sexual bias.

However if a woman does find herself in a relationship with a *narcissist* then she is likely to be on the receiving end of some very unhealthy and even emotionally damaging behavior.

Here are TWENTY signs that the man you're dating may be a narcissist.

1. He loves to talk about himself; many of his statements begin with the pronoun *"I."*
2. He manipulates others and lies.
3. He is overly jealous and believes others are jealous of him.
4. When something goes wrong, he blames everyone except himself.
5. He loves to brag about himself and about his accomplishments.
6. He is critical and judgmental.
7. He cares too much, about what others think of him.
8. He never asks about how you feel.
9. He is too competitive, even about superficial things.

10. He always has to be "right" or have the last word.
11. He is into appearances and overly concerned about image and status.
12. He enjoys playing the role of victim even when he is not.
13. He does not take your needs seriously.
14. He is overly controlling.
15. He is always fishing for compliments, and if he cannot get one he is more than willing to give himself one.
16. He devalues or minimizes the accomplishments and successes of others.
17. Regardless of the situation and who is involved, he always seems to find a way to make it about him.
18. He is not able to connect with the needs and feelings of others.
19. There is a lack of "emotional closeness" or connection in your relationship.
20. He refuses to apologize or accept blame for anything.

Not only can the narcissist be an incredibly infuriating individual to be around he can also be harmful to the emotional well-being of others. However, while this man should not be discounted as a potential mate or spouse, a woman needs to carefully weigh the pros and the cons of getting involved with this man.

Chapter 14: Codependent personalities

Codependency can be defined as, having an underdeveloped sense of self-esteem combined with an inappropriate caring for others and an inappropriate reliance on another's response in a negatively reinforcing way.

Codependent personality is not one of the ten currently recognized personality disorders. Codependency was considered for inclusion as a personality disorder in 1987 but the decision was made to not to list it in the DSM-III-R since many of the traits associated with codependency could be considered beneficial in occupational and social functioning.

Codependents are sometimes referred to as caregivers, fixers, or rescuers. Whatever the chosen label the behaviors and relationship patterns are the same. These people have learned to live their lives through others as a coping mechanism or worse, a survival technique. For these people being needed is synonymous with being loved. Rescuers are made not born. They are most often the result of being the child of an abusive or emotionally absent parent or primary caregiver. They are also the product of being in a relationship with an alcoholic or substance addicted individual.

The central theme of their relationship choices is, "If you need me, you will never leave me." As a result, they go in search of individuals that are broken, addicted, and needy. They always choose down in relationships. This gives them the upper hand and enables them to maintain some thin veil of self-esteem, something they are severely lacking. Rescuers have often suffered severe emotional trauma at the hand of an abusive parent incapable of providing the affection and emotional nourishment necessary in order to learn how to love in a healthy way. They were deeply wounded at their very core and they carry the scars of lovelessness and low self-worth.

"Just below the surface of every rescuer is a lost and rejected child that doesn't feel that who they are themselves is worthy of love."
— *Tigress Luv*

The term codependency has evolved over the years. It originally referred to someone who was addicted to or in a relationship with *an addict*. However, today the term is more closely associated with someone who grew up in a home with at least one alcohol dependent or emotionally absent parent and therefore adopted a dysfunctional view of themselves, primarily an underdeveloped sense of *Self* along with an inappropriate caring for others.

Melody Beattie is perhaps the nation's foremost authority on subject of codependency. Her groundbreaking best-selling book, *Codependent No More* introduced us to the term codependency in 1986. In her book, Beattie defines a codependent as, ***"A person who has let another person's behavior affect him or her, and who is obsessed with controlling that person's behavior."*** She goes on in her book to describe characteristics and behaviors that are common among codependents. Some of these characteristics are:

1. Think and feel responsible for other people's feelings, thoughts, actions, choices, wants, needs, well-being, lack of well-being, and ultimate destiny
2. Feel anxiety, pity, and guilt when other people have a problem
3. Feel compelled to help others
4.   Feel angry when their help isn't effective
5.   Anticipate other people's needs
6. Do things other people are capable of doing for themselves
7. Feel bored, empty, and worthless if they don't have a crisis in their lives
8. Believe deep inside that other people are responsible for them
9. Get superficial feelings of self-worth from helping others
10. Try to catch people in acts of misbehavior
11. Become afraid to let other people be who they are and allow events to happen naturally
12. Think they know best how things should turn out and how people should behave

Because codependents have a dysfunctional relationship internally (with themselves), they are prone to have dysfunctional relationships externally (with others). They try to fill the hole they feel inside of themselves with something or someone outside. They derive their sense of worth from people and things outside of themselves. They do this by attending to the needs of others, often ignoring their own needs. They enter into relationships with people who they see as needing care, fixing, or rescuing. In relationships caregivers constantly live with a powerful compulsion to give to others that which they never received.

Men like this often get involved with clingy, needy, emotionally unstable women. Women often fall prey to relationships with males they think have potential, only to be disappointed repeatedly. Although constantly frustrated they remain in these relationships because their "little girl" needs are being met. Once again, *"If he needs me he will never leave me."*

All of this is the cost of not resolving their deep emotional childhood wounds. A caring, mutually nurturing relationship is foreign to codependents. They have seldom received affection and love from an emotionally available parent, or have experienced love that was not accompanied by pain.

Common characteristics found in codependents:

- Inability to really know what normal is
- Judge themselves very harshly
- Low sense of self-esteem
- Hypersensitive to criticism
- Feeling the need to rescue, help, or fix others at the expense of their own well-being
- Thinking and worrying about other people's problems

- Feeling responsible for other people's feelings
- The need to please others
- Feelings of emptiness and unworthiness
- Belief that "being needed" is an essential component to any relationship.

"The heart and soul of codependence lies in the difficulty codependents have knowing what their feelings are and how to share them. Codependents seem to have the most difficulty experiencing feelings moderately; they feel little or no emotions or have explosive or agonizing ones." — Pia Mellody

So how can one tell if you are a codependent? Here are ten red flags to look for:

1. Do you become obsessed with fixing and/or rescuing other people?
2. Are you easily absorbed in the pain and problems of other people?
3. Do you try to control others?
4. Is it important to you to please others, even more so than yourself?
5. Do you do often do more than your share?
6. Are you always seeking approval from others?
7. Do you have a difficult time saying, "No"?
8. Would you do anything to hold on to a relationship?
9. Are you excessively loyal to others even when the loyalty is not deserved?
10. Do you feel overly responsible when it comes to meeting the needs of others?

Codependent people can benefit from meeting with peers in a group therapy or support-group setting. In fact, the support group Co-Dependents Anonymous (Coda) was developed based on the Alcoholics Anonymous.

Many codependents were once the child of an alcoholic parent. Moreover, while alcoholism in a parent is not the only source of codependency in children or adult children it is a leading cause. An alcoholic parent by definition is an emotionally absent parent.

Children who are the products of alcoholic parents will develop into what is known as "a parentified child." A parentified child is a child who is subconsciously given the role of meeting the emotional needs of the parent and other family members. In some cases, the child is used as a *"surrogate spouse"* and must assume the responsibility of meeting the addicted parents emotional needs. This is sometimes referred to as *"emotional incest."*

In 1983 Dr. Janet Woititz, published her groundbreaking bestselling book, *Adult Children of Alcoholics*. In her book, Dr. Woititz identified the unique plight faced by children who were raised in a family with an alcoholic parent. She went on to identify thirteen traits that are common in *ACoAs or* **Adult Children of Alcoholics:**

1. ACoA can only guess what normal behavior is (In the alcoholic household home life varies from 'slightly mad

to extremely bizarre')

2. ACoA have difficulty following a project from beginning to end (The alcoholism takes the priority, there is seldom an example of how to see a project through from beginning to end)

3. ACoA lie when it would be just as easy to tell the truth (Lying, covering up, and denying are central to the alcoholic household. Lies are told to protect the alcoholic.)

4. ACoA judge themselves without mercy (As the child of an alcoholic, you were constantly told that you were not good enough.)

5. ACoA have difficulty having fun (An alcoholic home is always on edge, always fearful; the atmosphere in the house is thick with stress and tension.)

6. ACoA take themselves very seriously (As a child in an alcoholic home, you do not have a lot of fun. There was not room for spontaneous fun.)

7. ACoA have difficulty with intimate relationships (To be intimate, to be close, to be vulnerable, contradicts all the survival skills learned by children of alcoholics when they were very young.)

8. ACoA overreact to changes over which they have no control (If plans change outside of their control, that they will therefore lose control of their lives.)

9. ACoA constantly seek approval and affirmation (Mixed messages from childhood leave adult children of alcoholics very confused. 'Yes, No, I Love You, Go Away' were the messages you received.)

10. ACoA usually feel that they are different from other people (You never developed the social skills necessary to feel comfortable in a group.)

11. ACoA are either super responsible or super irresponsible—there is no middle ground (You either do it all, or do nothing.)

12. ACoA are extremely loyal, even in the face of evidence that the loyalty is undeserved (Family members hang in long after reasons dictate that they should leave. The so-called "loyalty" is more the result of fear and insecurity than anything else is.)

13. ACoA are impulsive. They tend to lock themselves into a course of action without giving serious consideration to alternative behaviors or possible consequences. (When you were a child, you never had the chance to behave impulsively; you were forced to behave like an adult when you were a child. So as an adult, you may make

up for this loss.) Adapted from Adult Children of Alcoholics by Janet Woititz

Examples of movie/film characters with a Codependent personality:

- Jack Lemmon as Joe Clay and Lee Remick as Kirsten Arnesen, Days of Wine and Roses, 1962
- Lorraine Bracco as Mary, Radio Flyer, 1992
- Molly Ringwald as Andie Walsh, Pretty in Pink, 1986
- Meryl Streep as Sophie, Sophie's Choice, 1982
- Johnny Depp as Gilbert Grape, What's Eating Gilbert Grape, 1993

Chapter 15: Schizoid personality disorder

The term "schizoid" was coined in 1908 by Swiss psychiatrist Eugen Bleuler to describe a human tendency to direct one's attention inward and away from the external world. The behavior was much more than what is considered shyness or introversion. Bluer labeled the individuals who exhibited this type of extreme introversion *schizoids* or *schizoid personalities.*

Some have suggested that this disorder has its origin during the fetal stage when the child is still in the womb. A mother, who is under tremendous stress and conflict, perhaps with her spouse, while she is carrying this child, could transmit those negative feelings (chemicals) to the fetus.

These individuals are generally high functioning but simply do not care about friendships or romantic relationships. It is not as if they fear them, they simply are not interested in others with the exception perhaps of a pet.

There are two hallmark symptoms of this personality type and they are the avoidance of people and social situations and displaying little or no emotion (flat or blunted affect). People with schizoid personality disorder generally avoid all social contact including romantic relationships. Most are believed to be *asexual* meaning they have little or no interest in sex. In addition, they demonstrate little in the way of emotions, either positive or negative. Remarkably they are generally unaffected by either praise or criticism.

People with schizoid personality do not form close connections with others. The reason they avoid social contact is not so much that they are incapable; it is simply that they prefer their solitude. They find life to be less complicated and more fulfilling without other people. In addition they genuinely seem to be unaffected by what others may think, believe, or say about them.

Schizoid personality is diagnosed more often among males than in females; the overall prevalence of schizoid personality disorder is believed to be around one percent of the adult population.

It is important to differentiate this disorder from social anxiety disorder, social phobia, or avoidant personality disorder. People with social anxiety and avoidant personality do desire relationships and being in social situations, they just find it to be extremely difficult. The schizoid however has no such need or desire.

Common thoughts of people with Schizoid personality:

- *My life is less complicated without other people.*
- *Other people's opinions do not matter to me.*
- *I feel better off being left alone.*
- *Romantic relationships are not important to me.*
- *I genuinely prefer doing things on my own than with others.*
- *I do not care what others may think or say about me.*
- *I prefer to live within my inner fantasy world rather than live in the outside world.*

Like most personality disorders, schizoid personality manifests itself by early adulthood through social and emotional detachments. Individuals with this disorder are able to function in everyday life, but will not develop any meaningful relationships with others.

Austrian psychoanalyst Wilhelm Reich said of these individuals:

"The schizoid child essentially perceived or experienced their earliest life, from conception till birth and beyond, as a hostile reception where they were rejected not just in their own nature and humanity, but for existing at all. The child felt threatened and unsafe, and may have wanted to die rather than continue in life."

They are loners, daydreamers, aloof, and indifferent. They will however often develop attachments to animals. They do well at solitary jobs which others might find intolerable. There is evidence indicating that schizoid personality disorder may lead to a mild form of schizophrenia. People with schizoid personality disorder, are not psychotic however, they are often intelligent and very much in touch with reality unless they go on to develop schizophrenia.

Schizoid personalities prefer solitary activities and occupations. The work of nighttime security guard, lighthouse keeper, or working the graveyard shift would be ideally suited to them, although their interpersonal apathy and lack of initiative make it less likely that they would succeed at any job. They prefer mechanical or abstract activities to those that involve working with other people. Often, they drift into marginal living arrangements, such as skid rows, cheap hotels, and rundown boarding houses. Although they may passively accept sexual attention from others, they are typically indifferent to potential romances or friendships.

According to the Psychiatric DSM 4th edition, four of the following symptoms must be present in an individual in order to receive a diagnosis of schizoid personality disorder:

1. Neither desires nor enjoys close relationships, including being part of a family
2. Almost always chooses solitary activities
3. Has little, if any, interest in having sexual experiences with another person
4. Takes pleasure in few activities
5. Lacks close friends or confidants other than first-degree relatives
6. Appears indifferent to the praise or criticism of others
7. Shows emotional coldness, detachment, or flattened affect

Like all personality disorders, there is no "real" cure for schizoid personality disorder; therapy that accomplishes a long-term level of trust may be useful in certain cases of schizoid personality. However schizoid individual will rarely seek out the help since they are perfectly content living the solitary life that they live. The fact that their lives are free from romantic partners, family, and friends, makes it even more unlikely that they will seek treatment.

Examples of movie/film characters with Schizoid personality:

- Anthony Hopkins as butler James Stevens, Remains of the Day, 1993
- Ralph Fiennes as Count Laszlo de Almásy, The English Patient, 1996
- The Batman character as well as his alter ego Bruce Wayne in the Batman movies

Chapter 16: Avoidant personality disorder

Avoidant personality disorder, abbreviated as AvPD, is sometimes referred to as anxious personality disorder and it is believed to affect men and women in equal numbers. Estimates of its prevalence range from two to five percent of the adult population.

"Individuals with AvPD view the world as unfriendly, cold, and humiliating. People are seen as potentially critical, uninterested, and demeaning; they will probably cause shame and embarrassment for individuals with AvPD. As a result, people with AvPD experience social anxiety and are awkward and uncomfortable with people." Millon & Davis, 1996

For people who suffer with AvPD extreme shyness and fear of rejection make it extremely difficult to interact with others socially and professionally. These unfortunate individuals are not simply shy; they are crippled by extreme feelings of inadequacy and self-loathing. Their feelings of inadequacy have permeated every aspect of their lives leaving them lonely, depressed, and often isolated.

People with AvPD are uncomfortable and restrained in social situations, overwhelmed by feelings of inadequacy, and extremely sensitive to negative criticism. They are often so fearful of being rejected that they give no one an opportunity to reject or accept them. People with this disorder believe themselves to be unappealing or inferior to others. They exaggerate the potential difficulties of new situations and seldom take risks or try new activities. They often feel alone and depressed. As a result, some people with this personality disorder develop an inner world of fantasy and imagination.

In order to receive a diagnosis of AvPD the Psychiatric DSM 4th edition states that at least four of the following seven criteria must be met:

1. Avoids activities that involve interpersonal contact
2. Avoids getting involved due to a fear of not being liked by others
3. Restraint in intimate relationships due to a fear of shame or ridicule
4. Marked preoccupation of being rejected or criticized by others
5. Stays away from new interpersonal situations due to feelings of inadequacy
6. Views oneself as inferior, socially inept, or personally unappealing
7. Takes few if any personal risks in the engagement of new activities, for a fear of being embarrassed

Common thoughts of people with AvPD:

- *People will reject me if I allow them to get close to me.*
- *If I expose myself to others, they will be critical of me and ultimately reject me.*
- *When in social situations I need to keep myself as inconspicuous as possible.*

- *Rather than try something new and fail, it is better not to even try.*
- *I cannot handle myself in social situations.*
- *People do not like me.*
- *If I allow myself to be vulnerable people will hurt and reject me.*

The cause of Avoidant Personality Disorder is unknown. However, like other personality disorders it is believed to have a genetic, a psychological, and a social component. Many people diagnosed with AvPD have had painful early experiences of chronic parental criticism or rejection. A combination of genetic traits and child abuse/neglect is most often associated with the disorder, but no conclusive study exists.

Like all personality disorders, the long-term outlook for these patients is generally not good. However, antidepressant and anti-anxiety medications can often provide symptom relief and reduce the sensitivity to rejection. Psychotherapy, particularly cognitive-behavioral approaches, can also be helpful. A combination of medication and talk therapy may be more effective than either treatment alone. Avoidant personality disorder is perhaps the most responsive to treatment of all of the personality disorders we have discussed in this book.

Examples of movie/film characters with Avoidant personality disorder:

- Woody Allen as Leonard Zelig, Zelig, 1983
- Andie MacDowell as Ann Bishop Mullany, Sex Lies and Videotape, 1989

Chapter 17: Histrionic personality disorder

The word histrionic comes from the Latin word, *"histrio"* meaning actor or performer. People with HPD or histrionic personality disorder are extremely emotional; they are typically described as *emotionally charged* and continuously seek to be the center of attention. Their exaggerated rapidly changing moods can be a major source of distress for both themselves and for those around them. Individuals with histrionic personality and borderline personalities share many of the same behaviors. However, it is the overtly sexual behavior of the histrionic, which makes them much different.

People with HPD are always *on stage,* using theatrical gestures and mannerisms and grandiose language to describe ordinary everyday events. They are constantly changing themselves to attract and impress an imagined audience and in the process change not only their surface characteristics but also their opinions and beliefs. In addition, their speech tends to be lacking in detail and substance.

"Childhood trauma might be a trigger for HPD in some cases. The children who experience trauma from abuse to natural disasters undergo changes in brain chemistry affecting regions that make them moody, oversensitive to stimulation, and unable to accurately assess certain social and environmental cues. Childhood neglect could also be a factor, experts in the field believe. If parents or guardians habitually ignore, discount or dismiss a child's

92

thoughts, feelings and experiences, the child may decide that dramatic presentations from dressing provocatively to telling stories of wild adventures or crises—are necessary to get attention." Bruce Perry, M.D.

The prevalence of HPD in the general population is estimated to be approximately three percent. Clinicians tend to diagnose HPD more frequently in females; however, when structured assessments are used to diagnose HPD, clinicians report approximately equal prevalence rates for men and women.

People with HPD sometimes draw attention to themselves by exaggerating a physical illness. They often behave provocatively and try to achieve their goals through sexual seduction. Most obsess over how they look and how others will perceive them, often wearing bright, eye-catching or sexually provocative clothes.

They exaggerate the depth of their relationships claiming to be intimate friends with the most casual of acquaintances. They often become involved romantically with partners who may be exciting but who do not treat them well. They are vain, self-centered, demanding, and unable to delay gratification for long; they overreact to any minor event that gets in the way of their quest for attention.

HPD would seem to have a unique position among the ten personality disorders in that it is the only personality disorder explicitly connected to a patient's physical appearance. Researchers have found that HPD appears primarily in men and women with *above average looks.*

Individuals with this disorder may have difficulty achieving emotional intimacy in romantic relationships. They may seek to control their partner through emotional manipulation or seductiveness on one level, while displaying a marked dependency on them at another level.

"In the 2012 child molestation case involving the State of Pennsylvania versus Penn State assistant football coach, Jerry Sandusky, defense witness and forensic psychologist Eliot Atkins testified after conducting a six-hour interview with Sandusky that the Penn State football coach met the criteria for HPD." CBS/AP, *June 20, 2012*

People with HPD often have impaired relationships with same-sex friends because of their sexually provocative behavior or their demands for constant attention. They crave novelty, stimulation, and excitement and have a tendency to become bored with their usual routine.

The exact cause of histrionic personality disorder is not known, but many mental health professionals believe that both learned and inherited factors play a role in its development. There is a tendency for HPD to run in families, which suggests a genetic component. However, the child of a parent with this disorder might simply be repeating learned behavior. Other environmental factors that might be involved include a lack of criticism or punishment as a child, positive reinforcement that is given only when a child completes certain approved behaviors, and unpredictable attention given to a child by his or her parents.

In order to qualify for a diagnosis for HPD a person must have five or more of the following eight symptoms.

1. They are uncomfortable in situations in which he or she is not the center of attention
2. Interaction with others is often characterized by inappropriate sexually seductive or provocative behavior
3. Displays rapidly shifting and shallow expression of emotions
4. Consistently uses physical appearance to draw attention to themselves
5. Has a style of speech that is excessively impressionistic and lacking in detail
6. Shows self-dramatization, theatricality, and exaggerated expression of emotion
7. Is highly suggestible, i.e., easily influenced by others or circumstances
8. Considers relationships to be more intimate than they actually are

Common thoughts of people with Histrionic personality:

- *In order to feel special and important I need to impress and entertain others.*

- *I feel empty when people ignore me.*
- *I need to be the center of attention in order to feel valued.*
- *I cannot tolerate the feeling of being bored.*
- *Receiving attention makes me feel special and fills my emptiness.*

Medication does little to affect the course of HPD, but may be helpful with symptoms such as depression and anxiety. Long-term psychotherapy has shown to be modestly beneficial. Like most personality disorders, histrionic personality disorder typically will decrease in intensity with age, with many people experiencing few of the extreme symptoms by the time they are in the 40s or 50s.

Movie/film characters with Histrionic personality disorder:

- Scarlett O'Hara played by Vivien Leigh in Gone with the Wind, 1939
- Austin Powers played by Mike Myers in the Austin Powers movies of the 1990s
- Blanche DuBois played by Vivien Leigh, Streetcar Named Desire, 1951

Chapter 18: Self-defeating personality disorder

Is it possible for us to be our own worst enemy? Do people get in the way of their own successes and when they do meet with success sabotage it in order to end it?

"There comes a point when you either embrace who and what you are, or condemn yourself to be miserable all your days. Other people will try to make you miserable; don't help them by doing the job yourself." — L. K. Hamilton

Given the choice between being happy and being sad, most of us would choose happiness, but not everyone. There are people who thrive on being sad. The simplest way to describe this is that some people want or need to be sad, and they will devise ways of making that happen.

When a person habitually undermines himself or is drawn to situations or relationships where he/she will be disappointed, or be mistreated psychologists sometimes refer to this as SDPD or Self-defeating personality disorder. It was formerly known as *Masochistic personality disorder*. SDPD was considered for inclusion in the Diagnostic and Statistical Manual of Psychiatry in 1987 but was rejected as a diagnosis requiring further study. It was not including in the most recent version of the DSM released in 2013.

However, just because it is not in the DSM does not mean that it does not exist. This disorder can be defined as, *"a pervasive pattern of self-defeating behavior, beginning by early adulthood and present in a variety of contexts. The person may avoid or undermine pleasurable experiences, be drawn to situations or relationships in which he will suffer, and prevent others from helping him."*

To qualify for this diagnosis a person must exhibit at least five of the following eight behaviors:

1. Chooses people and situations that lead to disappointment, failure, or mistreatment even when better options are clearly available
2. Rejects or renders ineffective the attempts of others to help him
3. Following positive personal events, responds with depression, guilt, or a behavior that produces pain
4. Incites angry or rejecting responses from others and then feels hurt, defeated, or humiliated
5. Rejects opportunities for pleasure, or is reluctant to acknowledge enjoying himself
6. Fails to accomplish tasks crucial to his personal objectives despite demonstrated ability to do so
7. Is uninterested in or rejects people who consistently treat him well, e.g., is not attracted to caring sexual partners
8. Engages in excessive self-sacrifice that is unsolicited by the intended recipients of the sacrifice

People who suffer with this disorder adopt unrealistic goals and when they fail to achieve them, they react with anger, depression, rage etc. They are overly self-sacrificing, rejecting of those who treat them well, fail to finish important tasks, reject opportunities for pleasure, incite rejecting responses from others, reject help from others, and makes self-defeating choices of people and situations.

Although there is believed to be a genetic component involved, self-defeating behavior is believed to start in childhood with parents who fail to discipline a child effectively. There is disagreement on exactly what type of parenting causes this behavior to emerge. One theory is, that if a child receives an excessive amount of praise from a parent even when it is not deserved, then the children will grow up with an inflated image of themselves that they feel they must protect against realistic tests. They protect it by taking on a handicapping excuse.

Common thoughts of people with Self-defeating personality:

- *Being ambitious and competing with others is wrong*
- *I cannot tolerate being the center of attention.*
- *I cannot tolerate success or pleasure.*
- *The only way that I can gain inner peace is by losing sight of my own needs.*
- *I feel guilty when receiving special attention.*
- *I do not want others to do things for me; it makes me uncomfortable.*
- *I can only relax and indulge myself only when I am alone.*
- *I am unworthy and undeserving of love, attention, and pleasure.*
- *Advancing in my career is not important to me.*

- *I hate to ask other for help or favors.*

Another theory is that if a child is exposed to a strict authoritarian parent and has been repeatedly told that he does not deserve love or that he deserves pain then that is exactly what he will grow up to believe. As a result, he will avoid and reject anything that leads to pleasure. Even when there is pleasure, he can never enjoy it since he will be riddled with feelings of guilt and shame.

There is no medication to treat self-defeating personality disorder. However, long-term psychotherapy of any kind can be helpful. Regardless of the type of psychotherapy, it will require long-term treatment and it will be an uphill battle, because this type of patient will always remain invested in defeat.

Chapter 19: Dependent personality disorder

DPP or Dependent personality disorder is one of the three so-called, *anxious personality disorders*. People with dependent personality disorder exhibit a pattern of dependent and submissive behavior, relying on others to make decisions for them. DPD is diagnosed more often in women than in men.

People with this disorder have incredible difficulty with separation. They are devastated when a close relationship ends and will frantically seek out another relationship to fill the void. As a result, many will get involved in relationships where others either physically or psychologically abuse them. Because they are so fearful of rejection, they are overly sensitive to disapproval and keep trying to meet other people's wishes and expectations even if it means doing things they dislike.

"A person raised in a healthy family is equipped to live a confident and independent life; someone from an unhealthy family is filled with fear and self-doubt. The devaluing messages of control and manipulation create dependency so those who most need to leave their family of origin are the least equipped to do so." — *Christina Enevoldsen*

People with this disorder so lack confidence in their own ability and judgment that they allow others to make important decisions for them. They often rely on a spouse or a parent to decide where to live, where to work, and who to befriend.

Common thoughts of people with Dependent personality:

- *"I can't do it by myself."*
- *"I need someone to take care of me."*
- *"I need someone to tell me what to do."*

While there is most likely a biological predisposition for DPD, some researchers believe, an overprotective parenting style can lead to the development of traits in people who are susceptible to this disorder. Caretakers may encourage dependence in the child to meet their own dependency needs, and may reward extreme loyalty but reject attempts the child makes toward independence.

Dependent personality disorder signs and symptoms:

- Inability to make decisions
- Passivity
- Avoiding personal responsibility
- Avoiding being alone
- Devastation or helplessness when relationships end
- Unable to meet ordinary demands of life
- Preoccupied with fears of being abandoned
- Easily hurt by criticism or disapproval

According to the DSM of Psychiatry, five of the following eight symptoms are necessary to qualify for a diagnosis:

1. Has difficulty making everyday decisions without an excessive amount of advice and reassurance from others
2. Needs others to assume responsibility for most major areas of his or her life
3. Has difficulty expressing disagreement with others because of fear of loss of support or approval
4. Has difficulty initiating projects or doing things on his or her own (because of a lack of self-confidence in judgment or abilities rather than a lack of motivation or energy)
5. Goes to excessive lengths to obtain nurturance and support from others, to the point of volunteering to do things that are unpleasant
6. Feels uncomfortable or helpless when alone because of exaggerated fears of being unable to care for himself or herself.
7. Urgently seeks another relationship as a source of care and support when a close relationship ends.
8. Is unrealistically preoccupied with fears of being left to take care of himself or herself.

Complications to this disorder may include depression, alcohol and drug abuse, and susceptibility to physical, emotional, and sexual abuse. Psychotherapy is the preferred form of treatment for people with dependent personality disorder. Medication may be helpful to treat other underlying conditions. With treatment, many people with DPD will experience some improvement.

Certain types of drugs such as antidepressants and sedatives are often prescribed for to treat symptoms of anxiety and depression. Like many personality disorders, dependent personality disorder, will sometimes lessen in intensity as the individual ages.

Examples of movie/film characters with Dependent personality:

- Buster Bluth played by Tony Hale in Arrested Development, 2003
- Hedra Carlson played by Jennifer Jason Leigh in Single White Female, 1992

Table 1

Personality	Prominent symptoms	Prognosis/Treatment
Borderline	Abandonment fears, mood instability, impulsive, self-harming, rage	Cognitive behavioral therapy, dialectical behavior therapy, medication for symptom relief
Narcissistic	Grandiose, lack of empathy, need for admiration, rage	Treatment resistant
Histrionic	Attention-seeking, dramatic, flirtatious, impulsive	Talk therapy can be helpful as well as medications to treat symptoms of anxiety and depression.
Schizoid	Aloof, indifferent to praise or criticism	These individuals rarely seek treatment
Avoidant	Socially inhibited, highly sensitive to criticism, feelings of inadequacy	Talk therapy can be helpful for these individuals as well as anti-anxiety medications.
Dependent	Inability to make decisions, highly dependent on others, submissive	Long-term talk therapy is helpful to some.

Table 2

The *American Psychiatric Association* organizes the TEN personality disorders into three clusters or groups

Cluster	Behavior	Personalities
A	Odd Eccentric	Schizoid Schizotypal Paranoid
B	Dramatic Emotional Unpredictable	Borderline Narcissistic Histrionic Anti-Social
C	Anxious Fearful	Avoidant Dependent Obsessive-compulsive

Conclusion

While no one is suggesting that all children who are the victims of abuse or neglect will go on to develop a clinical personality disorder, the link between the two is undeniable. Moreover, while it is true that most will not develop a personality disorder, the fact is many will develop some type of emotional or mental health problem as an adult. This includes things such as Depression, Anxiety, PTSD, eating disorders, and substance abuse disorders.

Many things go into an individual developing a clinical personality disorder; this book has suggested a *biopsychosocial* model. That is the coming together of a child's biology (genes from the mother and the father), the child's psyche (the temperament and disposition of the child), and social factors (the environment the child experienced particularly during the first three years). The data suggests that approximately nine percent of these vulnerable children will go on to develop a personality disorder as adults.

The conventional literature regarding personality disorders suggests that by their very nature (*ego-syntonic*) they are treatment resistant. And, while this may be true, it does not mean that improvements cannot be made in courageous individuals who have insight into their condition and a genuine desire to improve. We know that the treatment for borderline personality disorder has improved dramatically over the last fifteen years largely because of the remarkable work of American psychologist Marsha Lineman and the introduction of her Dialectical Behavior Therapy (DBT). In addition, the introduction of selective serotonin reuptake inhibitors (SSRIs) in the 1980s and atypical antipsychotic medications in the 1990s have been significant in terms of symptom relief for those with BPD and other personality disorders. Therefore, there is hope for those who seek it, and there will likely be better treatments and medications in the future.

It is important to remember that the disorders discussed in this book, clinical personality disorders, are very real. The individuals who suffer with these disorders have biologically observable differences in certain regions of their brains. Therefore, they are based on medical science, particularly neurology.

Currently there is no cure for a clinical personality disorder. There are however effective treatments, both pharmaceutical and talk based therapies can be helpful in many cases. Of course, *insight* on the part of the individual is the first step in the treatment of these conditions since we cannot fix that which we do not first acknowledge. Insight simply means that an individual recognizes that they have a problem. Insight sounds like this, *"I have a problem!"*

Insight is a huge first step but it must be followed by desire and courage in order to bring about change or healing. If insight is, *"I have a problem"* then desire is, *"I want something better."* Moreover, courage is, *"I am willing to do whatever it takes to get better!"* When we combine these three powerful forces, insight, desire, and courage then the possibility for genuine improvement and healing can begin.

There is no such thing as a perfect parent, and even parents with the best of intentions, make mistakes in childrearing. However, there is a big difference between falling short in the parenting process and intentionally or unintentionally perpetrating neglect or abuse upon a child. The former is frequent and is certainly forgivable; the latter is less common and is indefensible. Fortunately, most parents are able to get it right simply by following their instincts and practicing the philosophy *"do no harm."*

19th Century abolitionist and writer Frederick Douglass famously said, *"It is easier to build strong children than to repair broken men."* This quote, as much as any, epitomizes the theme of this book. Children who come into the world with emotionally healthy, attentive, loving parents have a very good chance of living happy productive lives. However, when parents are lacking in essential elements of themselves, things such as self-love, empathy, and the ability to connect with and nurture their children, the children will always suffer. Oftentimes the price the children will pay for the parents' deficits will be very high.

John Bradshaw is a bestselling author, theologian, and family counselor. He has written extensively on families, parenting, shame, codependency, and healing. With respect to parents and the role of an effective parent, Bradshaw said:

"The job of parents is to model. Modeling includes how to be a man or woman; how to relate intimately to another person; how to acknowledge and express emotions; how to fight fairly; how to have physical, emotional, and intellectual boundaries; how to communicate; how to cope and survive life's unending problems; how to be self-disciplined; and how to love oneself and another. Shame-based parents cannot do any of these. They simply don't know how." — John Bradshaw (Healing the Shame that Binds You)

This book examined seven clinical personality disorders *borderline, narcissistic, histrionic, schizoid, avoidant, dependent, and self-defeating.* In addition, we examined a personality type known as *codependent personality.* All eight of these are in part the result of some form of abuse/neglect experienced during childhood most often at the hand of an ineffective or abusive parent or caregiver. Again, there are certainly other factors at play in the development of these disorders, most notably genetics.

These disorders have been with us for longer than psychiatry has begun studying them and there is no reason to believe that they will be eradicated anytime soon. As long as there are parents who fail to nurture, protect, love, and honor their children, there will continue to be an unfortunate number of children who will grow to become adults with damaged or *wounded personalities.*

Glossary of terms

Abandonment fears: This is the hallmark trait of BPD but it also applies to many others. It is the intense fear, based on early childhood experiences, of being abandoned, left alone, or rejected by a loved one or partner.

Adolf Stern: The American psychoanalyst who coined the term borderline.

Asexual: Having little or no interest in sex. Schizoid personalities are generally thought to be asexual.

Attachment: The manner in which an infant bonds with its mother during its first year of life.

Attunement: The reciprocal nonverbal communication that occurs between a mother and her infant that has profound effects on the child's emotional development.

Benign interpretation: A coping mechanism whereby individuals learn to interpret events as benign or neutral as opposed to malicious and catastrophic.

Big Five Theory: The most widely accepted theory of human personality; it proposes that there are five broad dimensions to human personality: openness, conscientiousness, extraversion, agreeableness, and neuroticism.

Biopsychosocial: A theory, which proposes that personality disorders are the result of a combination of genetics, child temperament, and early childhood experiences.

Black and white thinking: Also known as dichotomous thinking, it is the manner in which borderlines and narcissists often see the world, all good or all bad.

CBT: Cognitive behavioral therapy, a highly effective form of talk therapy whereby individuals are encouraged to challenge their negative thoughts

CODA: Codependents Anonymous, a 12-step type support group for codependents.

Codependent: An individual who has a dysfunctional relationship with himself/herself and engages in unhealthy rescuing and caretaking behavior.

Core damage: A particularly devastating form a child abuse/neglect in which children did not receive the essential love and nurturing that is required to live a happy fulfilling adult life.

Daddy issues: Adult emotional problems that can be traced back to an unhealthy relationship with an absent or abusive father.

DBT: Dialectical behavior therapy, a type of psychotherapy developed in 1993 by psychologist Marsha Lineman specifically to treat patients with BPD.

Delusional jealousy: A form of jealousy that is common in those with BPD, and others, it is irrational and not based on real events.

Depersonalization: A feeling associated with severe anxiety or psychosis where an individual feels disconnected from oneself.

DSM: The Diagnostic and Statistical manual, considered the bible of psychiatry.

Ego-dystonic: A feeling that is inconsistent or goes against our psyche. Most psychiatric disorders including depression, anxiety, and ocd are ego-dystonic.

Ego-syntonic: Something that is consistent with ourselves, and feels comfortable to us. Personality disorders are ego-syntonic disorders.

Empathy: The ability to put oneself in someone else's shoes or feel another's pain. Empathy is considered one of the highest of all human emotions and it is notoriously lacking in clinical narcissists.

Gaslighting: A form of emotional abuse whereby an abuser will deny facts, events, and information causing the victim to question and doubt themselves. If done over a prolonged period it can cause an individual to question their reality.

Guilt: A healthy human emotion, which causes us to feel bad about something that we have done.

Idealization: An ego coping mechanism normally seen in children but also seen in borderlines and narcissists whereby individuals are elevated and seen as "all good."

Impulsive: The opposite of reflective, impulsive behavior is very common among those with BPD and HPD.

Inner child: A term used to describe our deepest wounds, it is the place inside of us where our most basic primal needs live.

Insecure attachment: A type of attachment where the mother fails to successfully bond with her infant during its first year. Depending on the severity, it can have severe repercussions for the child's emotional development.

Invalidation: A form of a child abuse, whereby a parent fails to acknowledge and respond to a child emotionally.

Lewis Goldberg: A 20th century American psychologist credited with developing the Big Five theory of personality.

MBPD: Male borderline personality disorder

Mommy issues: Adult emotional problems that can be traced back to an unhealthy relationship with an absent or inattentive mother.

Narcissistic injury: Any slight or criticism, which causes the narcissist to suffer emotionally. The psychological damage to the narcissist can be severe.

Narcissistic supply: The mechanism by which the narcissist gets his need for admiration met. A spouse is often used by the narcissist as his primary source of narcissistic supply.

Neurotic: A general term used to describe someone who tends to be emotionally unstable and as a result experiences mood swings, anxiety, and depression.

Projection: An ego defense mechanism whereby an individual denies their own distressing thoughts or feelings and places them on another .

Prophecy fulfillment: The human tendency to engage in behaviors that will reinforce what we already believe to be true about ourselves.

Psychiatrist: A medical doctor who specializes in the treatment of mental disorders.

Psychologist: Someone who studies human behavior and mental processes; he/she may or may not treat patients.

Psychotic: A psychological state whereby an individual loses touch with reality.

Rage: Anger which is out of proportion, it is commonly seen in both borderlines and narcissists.

Reparenting: A form of therapy for individuals with core damage issues whereby they are essentially parented a second time as adults either by themselves or by a therapist.

Secure attachment: A healthy bond that forms between a mother and infant during the first year of life.

Self-injury: Self-destructive behavior common among those with BPD, which includes self-cutting and self-burning.

Shame: One of the most disturbing emotions a person can experience, it has been called the hiding emotion and can lead a person to feel inadequate about *who they are.*

SSRI: Selective serotonin reuptake inhibitors, a safer class of antidepressant medications introduced in the 1980s they are also effective for anxiety.

Toxic shame: A particularly destructive form of shame experienced during childhood that can endure for a lifetime.

Traits: Symptoms or characteristics of a personality disorder, without having the full-blown disorder.

Triangulation: An abusive tactic whereby the abuser will avoid the victim and seek out a third party in order to garner support and further isolate the victim.

Acknowledgements

I would like to acknowledge the following individuals whose work has contributed to my knowledge of psychology, psychiatry, and the information in this book. These individuals have not only inspired me to write this book but they have assisted me on my personal journey of knowledge, insight, and healing.

- Edward Livingston Hicks, M.D
- Brené Brown, Ph.D.
- Shari Schreiber, M.A.
- Darlene Lancer, M.A.
- Sandra Hart, Ph.D.
- Deepak Chopra, M.D.
- Dr. Wayne Dyer
- John Bradshaw, *Healing the Shame that Binds You*
- Melody Beattie, *Codependent No More*
- Dr. Janet Woititz, *Adult Children of Alcoholics*
- Randi Kreger, *Psychology Today*, BPDCentral.com

I would also like to acknowledge the following sources for statistics and material used in the writing of this book:

Department of Health & Human Services, 2013
The Diagnostic and Statistical Manual of Psychiatry, DSM-IV
Adult Children of Alcoholics, Dr. Janet Woititz
Codependent No More, Melody Beattie
The American Psychiatric Association, www.apa.org

Goodreads.com, Goodreads Inc. 2016

Ptypes.com, 1998-2013, Dave Kelly

IMDB, Internet Movie Database, 1990-2016

About the Author

 Gregory Pacana was born and raised in Philadelphia, Pa in the Northern Liberties section of the city and currently resides in Fishtown. He is an avid reader, writer, and student of both psychology and psychiatry. He has been studying psychology formally and informally for nearly twenty years.

He has been a contributing writer and reporter for the *Philadelphia SPIRIT*, the *Philadelphia STAR*, and the *Philadelphia Public Record* newspapers. He has written over 200 articles on human behavior for the online *EXAMINER* platform. Gregory sits on the Patient Safety Committee at North Philadelphia Health Systems (NPHS).

Gregory's life took an unusual turn in 2007 when he decided to explore the growing world of online dating. He frequently found himself getting involved with a certain type of woman. These women tended to be very sensitive, romantic, and exciting. However, they also displayed dramatic mood swings, anxiety, jealousy, bouts of anger, and a tendency to self-medicate with alcohol.

He would later discover that many of these women suffered with a complex psychiatric condition known as *borderline personality disorder.* More so than any other single experience it was his encounters with these women and the powerful and sometimes damaging effect they had on him that drove him to begin studying psychology and in particular personality disorders. Later he would discover that he too possessed *"borderline traits."*

Gregory maintains a FACEBOOK fan page, **Fans of Human Behavior**, dedicated to the exploration and celebration of *positive psychology* with nearly 8000 followers. He can also be found on Twitter at *@gppacana.*

When Gregory is not researching or writing he can often be found in the many local bars, pubs, and restaurants in Fishtown and Northern Liberties watching his beloved Philadelphia Eagles or talking about sports, movies, politics, and current events.

Printed in Great Britain
by Amazon